This book is available at a special discount when ordered in bulk quantities. For information, contact Pusateri Consulting and Training at 716/631-9860 or www.pusatericonsulting.com.

This publication is designed to provide accurate and authoritative information in regard to the subject matter covered. It is sold with the understanding that the publisher and author are not engaged in rendering legal, accounting, or other professional services. If legal advice or other expert assistance is required, the services of a competent, professional person should be sought.

ISBN number 0-9716056-0-2

Printed in the United States of America

mirror mirror on the wall
am i the most valued of them all?

Leo J. Pusateri

The key to Leo's success is not his coaching skills or his knowledge of the financial services world, but his deep respect for –and interest in–the individuals he coaches. Leo has a keen eye for what makes each person unique. I have watched him masterfully moderate discussions in virtual classrooms where million-dollar producing financial consultants in Singapore coach their peers in Paris. His passion for helping people discover and articulate their uniqueness is infectious. He has an exceptional ability to simultaneously push to exhaustion and exhilarate and inspire the professionals he coaches.

His Value Ladder is a stunningly simple concept. At the same time, it is completely comprehensive. By completing and internalizing one's own Value Ladder answers, one is completely armed to answer any question a prospective client may have. Needless to say, this skill lifts a great burden off of the shoulders of any salesperson who wings answers. Leo's program takes the stress out of selling, and replaces it with enjoyment and confidence.

As financial products become more similar and less easy for consumers to distinguish, it becomes more important for financial advisors to distinguish themselves as individuals. Leo's work provides a roadmap for financial professionals to turn the challenges of a crowded marketplace into an opportunity to stand out from their competition.

It is an honor to have Leo as a strategic partner.

– Giles Kavanagh, Director
Sustained Learning Programs, Horsesmouth, LLC

Advisors cannot really differentiate themselves based upon product–name and brand, possibly to an extent–but the real issue is the financial consultant himself. That's a message you want all of your advisors to deliver. Leo teaches you to "rock forward" and deal with it in a warm, friendly, authoritative manner.

Leo had a tremendous impact on helping to shape the culture of our firm in terms of our style of business and how we approach our customers. Maybe our culture would have gotten there without Leo, but I believe he helped expedite, shape it, and mold it. By participating in the seminars, the FCs walked out thinking, "This is the way I need to do business." And these FCs went back to their offices and shared what they learned with their colleagues.

– Joe Baxter, Sr. VP
IJL Wachovia, Private Client Group Administration

If I can help advisors to clearly articulate their value and what they offer to clients, it helps them get new business as well as retain their current clients. Leo has helped advisors "jump to the next level." He motivates them to really solidify what their service and value is for the affluent client.

I have seen a significant increase in the level of assets under management from the advisors I work with as a result of Leo's training. Leo's approach is an absolute "must" for advisors who want to build an even more successful business.

– Ron Howard, Exec. VP, Assante Asset Management

Leo's practice is built squarely on his values. His business model, which I have completely adopted, is to serve from the heart and the head. What one brings to a business relationship flows from what one offers from one's character.

There is a "Pusateri Culture" in the financial services industry. When talking with another professional, mention Leo's name. What usually follows is a conversation about integrity, depth, character, success, perseverance–and Leo's family.

What is so remarkable about Leo and his practice is his ability to reach out to financial advisors through the industry and around the world. Their needs, their desires to achieve personal and professional success become his mission, his Holy Grail.

– Tony R. DePaolo, Senior Relationship Manager
   CheckFree Investment Services

Sometimes in this business we get so close to a that topic we really need another set of "eyes." The result is an AHA or a WOW, especially if that set of eyes belongs to Leo.

Our business is a commodity. I can get a mutual fund, a stock, or a bond just about anywhere–from an internet page to an individual broker. And so it's the ability to articulate the value that the consultant–or the organization–brings to their client, and to deliver it in a consistent fashion that is very, very powerful. That's what Leo does so well.

– John Granzow, President
   CapTrust Financial Advisors, LLC

Of all the trainers and coaches I've known over the years, Leo's message is articulated the best. My group fell in love with him instantly. Whenever I feel like I am becoming disorganized, or I have too many interruptions, I immediately go over the seven steps of the Value Ladder. Sometimes I hear things coming out of my mouth and I think, "Where did that come from?" And I realize that it is Leo's message coming through loud and clear. Leo is the one who keeps that "drum beat" going in my head. Leo will not let you off the hook–he makes you accountable, and he does it in a good and kind way.

Leo has made me better because he has forced me to write down my thoughts and make them more succinct. He's given me a lot of ways to differentiate myself in a business I've been in for 19 years that is getting so commoditized. Sometimes I don't really feel that I am any different from any of my colleagues in this business, but when I am in "Pusateri World" I can explain myself better.

I've been to many different sales training classes, but as far as getting the value message real tight, Leo is the best. The message has been very consistent for as long as I've known him, and that's what I really admire.

– John Cunningham, Financial Advisor, UBS PaineWebber

Successful managed account business rests on clear articulation and execution of needs-based financial consulting and planning. This value proposition must be executed every day by all staff within a managed account business unit. Leo's work helped us create a vision for our team and impart the requisite training that every team member needs to carry out our mission when partnering with clients.

**– Prabal Gupta, Head of Managed Accounts
  Nicholas-Applegate Capital Management**

The financial services marketplace is crowded with able, hungry and well-capitalized competitors. Thriving at the corporate and individual practitioner level, now more than ever before, requires the ability, skill and commitment to distinguish yourself with prospects and clients in an ongoing fashion. Leo is helping to point the financial service industry in a direction that can help it create distinct, successful brands and meaningful, lasting value propositions for clients. For the individual practitioner, this will become a matter of survival. Read this book and get to work.

**– Barry K. Mendelson, CIMA, Senior Vice President
  Robert W. Baird & Co. Incorporated**

It's not just the presentations that Leo's done for us that we find so valuable–he really has a gift for helping advisors articulate what it is they are trying to communicate. Beyond getting up in front of a group of 50 or more people and getting them excited about the message, Leo takes individuals from their scattered thoughts to a clear and coherent vision they can communicate with "confidence, passion and speed." What is powerful is his ability to help others, and he does this with caring and enthusiasm for each individual.

What I've learned from him is that you just can't wing it. He doesn't wing it and he teaches us not to wing it by being confident and clear.

We are growing about 60-70% in revenues a year since about the time we started working with Leo. The brokers–having gone through the program–are better salespeople. And our people are more understanding of the brokers from working with Leo. He's been a big part of our group and the group identifies closely with him, and we've also been empowered by his values.

**– Bob Moore, Director of Consulting Services
   McDonald Investments**

Before I met Leo Pusateri I spent many hours and dollars refining my process, but I had never developed a game plan to effectively communicate the value of our services and why we were different. Through Leo's 7-step Value Ladder, I learned how to clearly articulate (with confidence and passion) the value I bring to the table for my clients and prospects. Leo has helped improve my professional stature in the eyes of others.

**– John C. Moshides CLU, President
   Moshides Financial Group, Inc.**

I believe it's critical for advisors–and this is the piece that is missing–to be clear in articulating their value.

We've noticed that the advisor's delivery of his or her true value now is much clearer to the client up front, as well as throughout the entire meeting, so the first impression has much more impact. Leo's process is a clarification process. You start to understand why investors can be so confused; it's because we are sometimes not clear ourselves. Through Leo's training, we now deliver our message confidently, passionately and without hesitation. Why would anyone not want to associate themselves with a person like this?

– Laurie Nardone, President
Private Wealth Management Advisory Group Inc.

People with the insight and passion that Leo Pusateri has will only come around two or three times in your career. When you cross paths with them, seize the opportunity! Absorb as much as you can and apply their wisdom to your business and your life.

– Stephen A. Saenz, President, Paragon Resources, Inc.

One of the hard facts about our "New Economy" is that clients can switch financial consultants with the click of a mouse. Never before has the need for a financial consultant to establish his/her client value been greater. Leo Pusateri helps ensure that as a financial consultant, you will not be "clicked" away as you learn to discover and articulate your value to your client base.

– John Kikta, Vice President
Service Integration, J.P. Morgan Chase & Co.

I had a pretty good piece of managed account business, and I was committed to chasing it almost exclusively, always tweaking and improving my style. So we spent a lot of time together in the beginning of my coaching sessions with Leo breaking down the basics: how I spoke to clients, how I talked about the consulting business, how I perceived myself, how I articulated my value. I began to make gradual changes.

I not only improved in all of those areas, but I also made a dramatic leap in how I viewed myself, which was critical. I also made some dramatic improvement in the "nuts and bolts" of the consulting process once I already had the client and our relationship was a committed one. Which means I improved my planning process and my presentation when the money managers were presenting to my clients. The process really became quite streamlined for me at that point. I really understood myself better as a consultant and improved my business style. It was all due to Leo's coaching.

Leo has a very special way about him, notwithstanding the fact that he has a "golden tongue." We should all be able to present to clients the way he does to us.

If I had never met Leo, I would probably be doing the same type of business, but I definitely would not be doing as good a job as I am now.

– Bobby Present, Financial Consultant
RBC Dain Rauscher, former tennis pro

I instantly liked Leo because of the way he went about asking questions and listening. But what really sets him apart is his ability to ask the right questions that get at the heart of the issue. Many consultants put band-aids on issues and if you don't find out what the real problems are with clients or with organizations, then you can't solve anything.

Leo helped a member of my team who manages a very large piece of the retail business. By proactively putting together a business plan and implementing it, and facing some real issues head-on, he helped him focus and grow the business rather than simply maintain it. I would say that this piece of the business grew about 20% in a really tough year (2000).

Leo's heart and soul come through in his teaching. Leo "lives" what he teaches.

**– Lori A. Van Dusen, CIMA, Sr. VP Investments
   Consulting Group Director, Salomon Smith Barney**

I came away overwhelmed by Leo's energy, enthusiasm and complete dedication to his discipline. That discipline is helping sales professionals discover their "Unique Value."

I believe that eloquence is not merely a person speaking glibly or smoothly as a result of mastering the subject matter. Rather, true eloquence is achieved by a person being mastered by the subject matter itself. Leo is the brightest shining star in the galaxy that is true eloquence. With a caring, thoughtful attitude, Leo teaches, pushes and cajoles his students towards excellence. By having each person discover their "Unique Value," Leo unlocks their potential in a way unlike I have ever experienced.

– Jim Vogelzang, President, Vogelzang & Assoc.

Leo understands that, increasingly, the FC must be the value added; yet, today, most financial advisors cannot articulate the values they address and manage. As commission brokerage rates continue to decline, we cannot assume clients understand the value we add. Nor should we assume they can discern high-level professional investment from administrative counsel. This is why Leo's message is so profound. Every firm and every advisor must re-invent themselves as the industry moves from trade execution to advice.

Leo's training program helps organizations and advisors alike become world-class competitors in the delivery and execution of professional investment and administrative counsel. Leo helps makes this difficult transition easier. We are enriched by his process to create our Unique Value Proposition.

– Stephen C. Winks, Publisher
Senior Consultant News Journal

Leo gives us the tools to build confidence. He makes you look inside so hard, and he really challenges you. Leo completely "takes you apart"–and you really need that to go to the next level.

Whether you are a wirehouse or a regional, most firms have products (or access to products) that everyone else has. So how do we differentiate ourselves? Leo challenges us to use the tools he provides to build our business correctly. I just wish there were a "few more Leos."

We are going to continue to use Leo's training.

– Ken Mathis, Director of Sales Strategies, Hilliard Lyons

A friend once asked who I would give credit to for helping to develop my character. To that end, I dedicate this book to the following:

To my late father, who I always will remember for his strong work ethic and his commitment to family, and to my mother, whose amazing love never ceases. They formed my core values in my early years. I've told many people that if my four children someday have the same love and respect for me that I have for my parents, then I will consider my role as a father a success.

To my best friend, life partner, and wife of 23 years, Ann. Many people have asked me to analyze my strongest traits or to pinpoint what is the single reason I have been successful. Without a doubt, it is Ann. You have made me a better man. Your extraordinary support of my work is something that I will always remember. Our children have a phenomenal mom and in my eyes, as beautiful as you are on the outside, you are even more beautiful on the inside. I love you and thank you for always being you.

To my children, Leighann, Laura, Elizabeth and Brett. As I've told many people when describing all of you, "I love them all the same and they all touch my heart in different places." I am proud to be your father.

This book is dedicated to you all for truly being the core of my life, my success, and my love.

A Special Thank-You to Three Other Valued Friends in My Life

First, to my good buddy, John Connelly. It was you, John, and your late father who encouraged me more than anyone to start my own business and to truly live my passion through my work. You believed in me more than I believed in myself. You were always there to help–financially, by hiring me and, more importantly, always there to listen, advise and to keep things in perspective. I am truly blessed to have you as a friend.

To my good friend, Father Joe Rogliano. It was you, "Joe Boy," who reconnected me back to my faith in God and encouraged me in your own way to seek stewardship opportunities. My life has grown with your friendship. Your inspirational thoughts of "do good things" and also "this is your time" resonate with me daily. You are a part of our family and I thank you for your contributions to my life.

And finally, to my writing coach, Sydney LeBlanc. You are an absolute expert in this business and I am so fortunate to have met you and to have you assist me with this writing. You made it fun. You kept me on task and you opened up your heart and soul to this project. You are a very special friend and this book would not have come to completion without your help. Thank you, always, for your contributions and more importantly, your friendship.

A C K N O W L E D G M E N T S

I never thought this section of the book would be the most difficult to write. The dedication and tribute to the three other valued friends in my life flowed easily from my heart and soul. I have agonized with this section because I have been absolutely blessed with many great friends and clients.

I would first like to thank my long-term assistant and office manager, Sue Allan. Your dedication, fun personality and loyalty are appreciated.

Thank you to my good friend and advisor, Susan Burton. You have always been there to help and your commitment and caring are phenomenal.

I also appreciate and value my other advisors and great friends, Joe Kronenwetter, Tony DePaolo, and Jeff Liebel. Your strategic help over the years is truly appreciated.

A special thank you to my strategic partner, Horsesmouth, and my day-to-day partner, Giles Kavanagh. Your expertise and, more importantly, your friendship, are unbelievably valued.

My accounting and legal team of Steve Berman, Paul Nesper and Kent Roberts give me continual expert guidance.

Steve Gresham of Phoenix Investment Partners and Jim Vogelzang of Vogelzang & Assoc. have hired and referred me on numerous projects. You guys are simply great to work with and I get better every minute I'm around you.

To my good friend Jerry Lojacono, who worked with me for four years. The additional support team over the years of Nettie Nitzberg, Donna Wolski, Pete Schwenk, and now Amy Metz, have all helped us in project work.

To other past strategic distribution partners who have represented and recommended our work: Dave Myers from Alliance Performance Systems, Mitch Fairrais from On The Mark, Rosemarie Nelson from Competitive Advantage, Steve Saenz from Paragon Resources and Lyn Fisher from Financial Forum (who also assisted us with proofreading this book). Your representation of our work and input to improve our process is much appreciated.

Dave Specker is a former client, current peer and great friend, who also encouraged me to start my business. Also, to David and Barbara Elias for taking the risk to hire me at Elias Asset Management, which further introduced me to the investment management and financial services community. Thank you.

Larry Chambers is a great financial industry writing coach who helped me get this project started and opened up my eyes to the publishing world.

Over the last ten years, there have been some significant moments of growth and re-invention. Jim St. Charles of McDonald Investments was my first client and introduced me to his peers around the country. John Cunningham at UBS PaineWebber (formerly J. C. Bradford) was one of my first private clients and has constantly contributed and challenged me to get our message out in different ways.

Joe Baxter from First Union Securities, (formerly Interstate/Johnson Lane) has been a mentor to me for years.

John Hoskins and Glenn Jackson, founders of The Advantage Performance Group, gave me an opportunity to grow and refine our process by giving us a forum for feedback.

Kathy O'Shaughnessy, Vice President and Managing Director of First National Wealth Advisory Services, challenged me to provide a venue to give committed financial advisors our complete Discovering Your Value process. Our successful retreats grew out of her influence.

Bruce Dyer from UBS PaineWebber is one of the finest branch managers and leaders in the financial service business. He provided the opportunity to implement our curriculum in the most optimal way within his branch.

Connie Chartrand from Merrill Lynch International provides constant encouragement and gave us the opportunity to complete our first worldwide online learning initiative.

James L. Selak from Zebra Design is my corporate identity partner who provided expert and creative advice and work for this book project. Your analysis and review also led to this unique book title.

Finally, to all my clients and you, the readers of this book. You have challenged my thinking and have supported me for almost ten years now. I stay committed and passionate about my work with the goal to continue to exceed your expectations for the next decade.

C O N T E N T S

September 11, 2001
changed our lives forever

As I walked into the conference room in Princeton, New Jersey to deliver a program for Merrill Lynch, I watched in horror with people around the globe as terrorists attacked our country.

I was born after the Pearl Harbor attack, so I was educated about these types of tragic events by my parents and from movies. I was in the third grade when President Kennedy was shot. I was on a business trip in Corning, New York when the market crashed in 1987. I was at the Cole Field House at the University of Maryland watching an ACC basketball game when the fighting broke out in Kuwait. We all remember where we were and who we were with for our life-defining moments.

There I was, 46 years old, married 23 years, father of four, help-lessly watching TV (just as you were, I'm sure), as we were being attacked by terrorists. I was sorrowful for the victims at the World Trade Center towers, the Pentagon and near Pittsburgh. I could only imagine the pain and the emotional trauma families were experiencing. As a frequent air traveler, I could only envision the thought processes of those passengers and staff on the hijacked planes.

Those poor souls who were taken from us, many at their desks surrounded by pictures of their spouses and children just as I am in my office. What could possibly be next? This and many more questions will haunt us for the rest of our lives. Thoughts, introspection and action that may, in time, give us answers.

Our society currently is undergoing serious introspection.

Recently on the Oprah Winfrey Show, Dr. Phil McGraw, a noted psychologist and regular guest, posed some interesting questions to the audience:

1. What did you think was important before September 11, but is not important now?
2. What did you neglect before September 11?
3. What do you pledge to make important now?
4. What would be left unsaid or undone if you lost a loved one today?
5. What must you do now to live to your new standard?

We are all asking ourselves questions we thought we had answers to. And that's what this book is all about. It involves undertaking tremendous introspection, with similar questions that begin with the words, "who," "what," "why," and "how." These thought-provoking questions are designed to help you look inward at your organization, your team and, most important, at yourself.

Perhaps the tragic events of September 11, 2001 will force you to re-think your future. This book will help you in your efforts to re-examine and re-assess all areas of your life and your business. **It's a book designed to help you discover your value.** It's primarily the value you provide your clients, but I promise you will see and experience greater life awareness through this unique process.

The process we teach is called, the Value Ladder™. It consists of seven simple, yet penetrating questions. This book will help you begin to develop answers to these seven questions. If you're reading this book, I congratulate you on being committed, dedicated, and serious about your business.

Over the years I have found that a lot of financial entrepreneurs just don't work hard enough on their unique and compelling story of value. Many have done okay and don't see the need -

the old, "if-it's-not-broke-don't-fix-it" theory. I prefer the adage that Robert Kriegel used for his book title, *If It Ain't Broke, Break It.* Now that sounds like the attitude of someone who is good, but wants to be great, or the attitude of someone who is already great and wants to be extraordinary. It is the attitude of someone who is already extraordinary and truly wants to be "the best they can be."

That was exactly the attitude of one of my lifelong heroes, former UCLA head basketball coach, John Wooden. Success as defined by this legendary coach is "peace of mind which is a direct result of self-satisfaction in knowing you did your best to become the best that you are capable of becoming." That is what this book is all about.

Success necessitates change, an open-mind, and hard work on the most important story for you to tell: the story of you and your value. Be prepared for intense introspection. Be prepared to critically assess the man or woman in your mirror. Get ready to climb your ladder of success, your very own personalized Value Ladder.

$\Big($ Welcome to the process of discovering your value. $\Big)$
Leo J. Pusateri

When I give my presentations, I like to have some fun with words and phrases. Many times I create my own lexicon to make the words more visual, thus making them more memorable—other times, I just borrow great words that really drive a point home. Throughout the book we refer to some of these terms, so I thought we should define them up front for you.

AHA!: The light bulb going on in your head; that feeling of wanting to pound your fist on the table and say, "I got it!" A key point that finally hits home to you; something you feel compelled to act on.

Articulate Your Value: The verbal ability and confidence to look someone eyeball-to-eyeball and expertly discuss how your solutions will help achieve their goals.

Beating Around the Bush: A kissing cousin to "dancing around the subject;" evading the issue.

Business Beliefs: Your philosophies; the compelling story of your business.

Business is First a Meeting of the Hearts; Then Business Becomes a Meeting of the Minds: You need to connect emotionally with an individual before you begin the process of connecting with them logically.

Changing Client: Everyone on the face of this earth is a candidate for your services; they are more informed, have greater choices, are more enlightened, have competitive options, etc.

Confidence: This is the complete understanding of who you are and what value you provide. It embodies your business approach and philosophy. You can't expect your prospects to make a confident and informed business decision if you aren't confident in your presentation.

Confidence Meter: A self-rating tool to measure the confidence you feel you bring to the table regarding various aspects of your work.

Conversational Proficiency: Knowledge in key areas important to your prospects/clients, which enables you to come across as expert and create an aura that you have your act together; people talk positively about you to others due to this trait.

Conversational Respect: Being expert at acknowledging, clarifying, confirming; appreciating another point of view.

Core Values: This is what you stand for; the list of emotional descriptors or qualitative characteristics that connects you to your client and enables you to have a meeting of the hearts.

Dancing Around the Subject: A kissing cousin to beating around the bush; you know what it's like listening to someone who does this. The opposite of straight and honest answers. No bull, please.

Differentiation: The ability to distinguish yourself at three levels: your organization, your solutions, and you/your team.

Estimated Lifetime Value: What your clients' estimated worth is over the potential lifetime of the relationship; calculated by using such factors as revenue, referrability and profitability.

Financial Entrepreneur™ (FE): Any financial services individual who positions integrated, seamless financial solutions to other individuals, families and/or institutions.

Financial Entrepreneur Impact Ladder™: A chart showing selling and consultative behaviors and the impact they have on the clients you covet.

Financial Malpractice: Positioning potential solutions before you have a good understanding of your prospect's potential objectives is an early sign of financial malpractice. Simply put, it's writing a prescription before proper diagnosis.

Going Forward in Your Chair™: The confident feeling that comes from being prepared. You feel unbelievably self-assured and can answer your prospect's/client's questions with ease. It's the feeling of taking an athletic posture into the world of conversational and respectful selling. You're ready. You're prepared. You're confident, and have a world-class answer to any prospect's questions…let's get it on.

In the Moment: Having the confidence to instantly change your course or direction. Usually caused by gut feel or intuition; an attitude of "let's go for it."

In the Safe: Client retention expression meaning your relationship is secure; your client is going nowhere, in essence, they're in the safe. Nice to know you have the combination, and your competitors do not… make the most of it.

Intuitive Feel: Your gut feeling; caused by your heart and head talking to you at the same time advising you of appropriate action.

Kissing Cousins: A close relative of another word; an affectionate term; a phrase used to describe something close to another, but not exactly the same.

Mirror in Your Life: Every day you should look into your mirror at the most important competitor you have to compete against that day…YOU. Constant introspection is required, and there's no better way to do it than by looking in your daily "mirror of life." The person who truly knows all the answers regarding your level of commitment and your level of expertise is the one looking back at you every morning.

Mr. or Mrs. Ideal: Any potential prospect to whom you may position your services. It could be someone you covet as a client; someone you would be proud to say is your client; and, definitely someone you would enjoy having as your client.

Net it Out: Just say it the way you feel; no sugar-coating, please.

On Top of Your Game: Athletes and star performers call it "being in the zone;" when every word out of your mouth and your corresponding actions are near perfection. The feeling that you can't do anything wrong.

Passion: It's the fire you feel within yourself. It's your level of conviction. You know you're expressing yourself passionately when you sell from your heart. You're expressing what you believe in. People can FEEL that. They can feel that glow that comes from within you. You've heard the adage, "For he to enkindle another, he himself must glow."

Passionate Advocates: Individuals who become your apostles; those so impressed with your value and the memorable experiences you've created for them that they can't wait to refer you.

Process: A system of operations or creating something; a series of actions, changes, or functions that achieve an end or result.

Real Value: The application of your value that ultimately delivers proven results to others. Results can be either qualitative or quantitative.

Seven Key Emotional Issues™: The seven key emotional issues that we all have: Challenges, circumstances, concerns, frustrations, opportunities, needs, and problems.

Smile In Your Stomach™: That wonderful feeling and sensation in your gut when you know you're prepared to answer a prospect's question. You're prepared and you're on top of your game. Respectfully, you can't wait for the prospect/client to finish his question to you because you've got a confident, world-class response for him.

Speed: Your lack of hesitation in response. You don't have that sinking feeling in the pit of your stomach when you're asked any of the Value Ladder questions. If I ask you what makes you different, can you answer me without beating around the bush?

9

Without giving me a different answer every time I ask?

The Best Way To Learn How To Sell Is To First Understand What It's Like To Buy: By feeling the emotions of your prospects, you can more effectively connect to them and have greater empathy throughout the entire sales and consulting process.

Umbrella of Distinction™: A visual metaphor; the top of the umbrella represents your organization, the spokes represent your solutions, the handle represents your team/you.

Unique Value Proposition™ (UVP™): A brief statement or paragraph that clearly and concisely captures the essence of what differentiates you from your competition. It is your compelling message delivered with such confidence, passion and speed that you will really feel on top of your game.

Value: The solutions you provide that help achieve your clients' goals; tangible and intangible benefits at the highest level.

Value Judgment Day: That moment in time when you're with a prospect and she's ready to make her decision based on the dialogue you've had with her. You've asked questions at an expert level to determine what she values; you have listened intently and processed those answers with unbelievable respect; and, you have answered questions regarding the value you will bring to the table for her consideration. Drum roll, please... will she select you or someone else? This is the Value Judgment Day.

Value Ladder™: A series of seven simple yet penetrating questions that prospects might ask (or are thinking) to help them make a decision regarding your value and your differentiation. Each Value Ladder question has a corresponding rationale, which encapsulates what prospects are looking for when they ask you these seven questions.

Value Zealot: A leader who practices what he preaches on the issues of competing on value. They lead by example, they challenge their troops, and they do everything in their power to create a culture of value.

Values: Qualitative characteristics that embody what you stand for. Values serve as emotional connectors with the client: passion, commitment, trust, respect, and value are my five core values.

Virtual File Cabinet™: The most important file drawer in your office, or better yet, in your mind; all Value Ladder answers are stored here for retrieval on demand, whenever and wherever you need them.

Virtual Screwdriver™: We bring a big screwdriver to all our retreats. A virtual screwdriver is a mental tool meant to serve as a reminder to constantly think about tightening up your answers. Constant tightening takes you from good to great to extraordinary...and ultimately to being the best you can be.

You are the Value™: An expression we use which reflects our highest conviction that the most important reason clients do business with you is because of the value you provide.

Winging it: Buying time for yourself; grasping for words; stammering; looking around the room; dead air space; inconsistency of thought.

World-Class: Describes a level of services that are as good as it gets. You believe that the services you provide are at this level and, more importantly, your clients believe it. Synonyms of the term world-class used throughout the book are: Black-belt, Top-Gun, Navy Seal, Army Ranger, among others.

Zipper on Your Chest™: Can you visualize having a zipper on your chest? Imagine pulling it down and searching within to find critical answers inside your heart and your soul. These are the answers that drive your passion.

No More

Winging

it: Buying time for yourself;

grasping for words; stammering;

looking around the room; dead air

space; inconsistency of thought.

– Leo J. Pusateri

Mirror, mirror on the wall... am I the most valued of them all?

Definitely not, my friend, if you're "winging it." You probably know what I'm talking about. It's that feeling of not being on top of your game. It's the sense of being unprepared. You can't stand that feeling, and you do everything possible to look a prospect straight in the eye with confidence. That's true whether you're presenting to a board, to a high net worth individual, or over the phone to a small business owner.

"That's right, Mr. Ideal," you think, "I'm prepared, I know my business, I know your business, and I'm on top of my game." That's not being arrogant, or cavalier, or condescending. It's demonstrating professional respect. It's feeling like an expert. "Go ahead, Mr. Ideal, ask me your questions. I'm ready. I need and want to know what you value so I can professionally align my value to yours." This is the opposite of "winging it."

I'll tell you a story about a successful Financial Entrepreneur™ (FE) who demonstrates how important it is to be prepared and to know how to articulate his value. This FE was successful in spite of the fact that, more often than not, he was winging it. But, it could have been so much easier for him.

Then the FE and his team lost a $10 million piece of trust and estate business to a major national competitor. The prospect was represented by a top law firm across the street from the FE's office, who recommended he also speak to another financial organization before he made his decision. The lawyers and the wealthy prospect were so impressed with the financial firm that flew in from out of town that the competitor was able to scoop the business right out from under the local FE.

The reality was that the competition had a dynamic and passionate presentation that delivered VALUE. They were not winging it. Ten million dollars! Put your best Austin Powers voice on THAT one.

It was a real wake-up call for the FE. He could have captured more assets, relieved his anxiety before meetings, and wouldn't have lost "sure" business to competitors.

This story further crystallizes the many challenges that key producers and FEs face today. It was a true wake-up call. My friend told me he couldn't believe that after 25-plus years in the business, after raising nearly $500 million in assets, and being in the top 1% of his firm that, in essence, he and his team were still "winging it!"

To begin this journey of "no more winging it" and of discovering your value, take a look in your mirror to begin the introspection. Ask yourself these questions to determine if you are winging it:

- Have I ever lost a piece of big business?
- Have I ever done an autopsy to find out why?
- Have I ever given a presentation during which I didn't deliver confident responses to typical questions regarding my value?
- Have I ever felt that I–or my team members–lacked passion in my/our responses?
- Have I heard answers from other team members and thought, "Where did that come from?"
- Have I ever felt myself hesitating to answer certain questions from my prospects? (I'd bet your prospects can feel your uncertainty more than you think they can.)

Losing business doesn't hurt as much if you can look in your mirror of life knowing you did your best. It still hurts, but not as much. That's life and we move on. But it hurts a lot when your identical twin in the mirror honestly appraises the situation and says, "You blew it! You weren't prepared, you weren't on top of your game. You were just winging it."

Ouch! Now that really hurts.

Winging it occurs when you're just not on top of your game. Think about it. If the most important thing you have to sell is yourself and the value you provide, why haven't you perfected your message?

Who Do You Admire?

Can you think of other professionals who have wowed you with their greatness–others you admire that you know don't wing it? These may be role models in the sports world like Tiger Woods or Michael Jordan. You may think of Bill Gates and Warren Buffet in the business world, or Tom Hanks, Julie Andrews, or Oprah Winfrey from the entertainment realm.

And as far as world-class organizations are concerned, you can't get any better than Nordstrom's and Ritz-Carlton.

These people and companies work hard to distinguish themselves. They are focused and precise. They don't cut corners. They create memorable experiences for you. They don't wing it. As a result, you spread the word about these people and companies to others.

Think of people, companies or teams *you* admire and begin your process of introspection. You can learn a great deal about how you want to conduct your own business by studying their strategies. This is a process of discovery and one that forces you to be reflective. It also challenges you to assess where you are now, where you'd like to go, and how to develop strategies to get you there.

If I called some of your prospects and clients, would they be as passionate about you to others as you are when thinking about some of your sports, business or entertainment icons? Are you that passionate to your clients? Are you so dedicated to your work and the client experience you've created that they are your fervent advocates? Can they feel the love for what you do and want to be a part of it? Do they feel you're so on top of your game that you clearly stand out in the crowd?

In my experience, I've noticed that more than half of all FEs wing it with their client presentations. They haven't spent enough introspective time to truly understand their value. Is this what you do?

If you answered "yes," do you know why you're winging it instead of delivering a consistent message to every prospect you meet? Could it be that you wing it because you don't know your value? Or that you don't know how to articulate it? Maybe it's because you don't take the time to develop a consistent message or critical questions to deliver to each prospect. Simply put, is it easier to just wing it?

If you've ever lost a big piece of business, and don't know why, you need to stop taking the easy way out and start your intro-spection process. You must critically challenge yourself to assess exactly where you are in your business and your life. For example, reflect on the progress of your career and how much you're earning. Take an honest appraisal of your asset growth and the growth of your skill sets. Measure your career by your ability to sell yourself today. You are the final judge. Only you can give yourself the honest answers you truly require for this introspection process.

For instance, if you're already a black-belt, then which level are you? Or, if you're already All-Pro, which team–first, second or third? Can you get better? Where will you be tomorrow? Where can you improve your positioning, your team and your company? Are there holes left to fill?

17

AHA-It's a Giant Lightbulb!

So, you say you already know about value. You know that today's clients are more sophisticated, that you need to diferentiate yourself, and that you need to go through an introspective process to change your life. Now you want me to SHOW you something, right? How about some "real" benefits? What will you walk away with after reading this book?

First–and most importantly–you will learn to answer the questions that will help crystallize your value, and to articulate those answers with **confidence, passion, and speed.**

But what do I really mean, and why is this so important to your skill set?

Confidence, passion and speed are the foundation upon which you build your own unique value. Once you master them, you're on your way to financial 'black-belt' or 'top-gun' status.

• **Confidence** is the complete understanding of the critical questions of distinction and knowing what value you provide. It embodies your business approach and philosophy. You can't expect your prospects to make a confident and informed business decision if you aren't confident in your presentation.

• **Passion** is the fire you feel within yourself. It's your level of conviction. You know you're expressing yourself passionately when you sell from your heart. You're expressing what you believe in. People can FEEL that. They can feel that glow that comes from within you. You've heard the adage, "For he to enkindle another, he himself must glow." When is the last time someone said to you, "I can see how much you really enjoy your work." "I can tell how much you love what you do." When people say these things to you, you know you're hitting a nerve and you've touched something inside that draws them to you.

• **Speed** is your lack of hesitation in response. This means you don't have that awful feeling in the pit of your stomach when you're asked to differentiate yourself. If I ask you a question regarding your value, can you answer me without beating around the bush? Without giving me a different answer every time I ask?

You also will learn how to articulate your answers by connecting emotionally with your clients and establishing a meeting of the hearts. This will lead to an effective meeting of the minds. This is a key tenet of all of my work. As far as the tangible benefits–those you can see, touch and feel–well, here are some: you literally will gather more assets, increase your revenues, talk to prospects with a different sense of who you are and what you're all about. Your clients will establish lifelong relationships with you.

Taking you through the Value Ladder process is my real value to you. I will challenge and guide you throughout the book. In the process, gigantic light bulbs should appear over your head. I want to hear you jump and shout loud AHA's throughout your reading.

When FEs say I have helped them to "better speak to prospects in ways I never thought I could" and "you helped me distinguish myself in such a way that I reached a new level of business" and "my confidence has increased. I'm talking to people at levels I've never talked at before. I'm controlling sales calls differently. I'm getting deeper emotionally with them," and "I'm at peace with myself after 20 years of thinking I was in the wrong business," well, those are the "rewards" that keep me going every day. Now, that's real value.

$$\left(\text{Let's start working on your confidence, passion and speed.} \right)$$

mirror mirror on the wall
am **i** the most valued
of them all?

CHAPTER ONE

So, What Is Your Value?

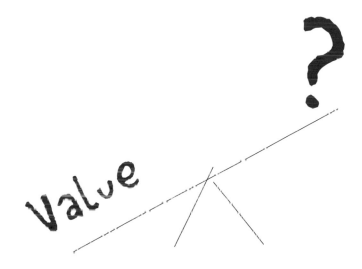

So, What Is Your Value?

The world is full of people
who know the price of everything,
and the value of nothing.

– Oscar Wilde

I remember growing up in the '60s and '70s watching the TV show, "Happy Days." It seemed like Fonzi could never admit he was wrong. He just couldn't get the words to come out of his mouth. Sometimes I find a similar thing happens to FEs. Many of them just can't seem to get the word 'value' out of their mouths, at least not without a lot of struggle.

So, I created a sound, simple, and compelling thought process to help you manage yourself through interactions with clients. A process that takes away the 'struggle.' I firmly believe this discovery and introspection will help you to fully understand and articulate your value in ways that you have never thought of. As Mack Hanan and Peter Karp stated in their book, *Competing on Value,* **"If you don't know your value, you can't sell your value."**

But, to properly answer the question, "What is Your Value?" you will first need to do some serious reflection and discovery, even if it causes some frustration and confusion. You will be challenged to look in your own mirror of life because all great learning processes involve these emotions. It doesn't matter whether you read this book from an organizational, a team, or an individual perspective. All that matters is that you are committed to go from good...to great...to extraordinary. You make the call.

I wrote this book for my own target market, which encompasses financial service organizations and/or individuals who position integrated, seamless and, many times, customized financial solutions to other institutions and/or individuals or families. I affectionately use the term "financial entrepreneurs™" to describe my clients. Why? Because as a company or as an individual in this business climate, we need to always think and act in the spirit of being a business owner.

It's important to have a world-class answer to the question, "What is Your Value?" and to do so requires being concise and ready to answer without hesitation. For example, my value to my clients is: **Empowering organizations and individuals to discover and articulate their unique value.** No winging it here. I'd better not be, or you may as well close this book now. In essence, that's my value. The real question for you as you embark upon this introspective process is: What is yours? What is your value?

You know the business scene today. Organizations are acquiring, consolidating, and merging at a frantic pace, all with the ultimate prize: becoming a client's financial partner and earning the coveted distinction of trust. The organizational mantras exist and the branding campaigns continue. The monumental message to the sales force is, "We can do it all." Or, "We do this better than others." Unfortunately, many *have it all*, but can't figure out how to *do it all.* Confusion exists at the client level as the global emphasis continues on a "full service, everything to everybody" mentality.

Time out.

One of the sales training courses I used to represent said it best. **The best way to learn how to sell is to first understand what it is like to buy.** What are clients experiencing? How difficult is it for them to make the right decisions? How can they sort through all the competitive options? As FEs, we all look the same, talk the same, dress the same, smell the same. That's what some of the changing clients are thinking about us. "Help me to understand how you are different and why I should do business with you," they say.

If you are a financial entrepreneur, then welcome to this unique process of introspection and discovery. If you are not an FE, welcome also. These are universal principles that apply to any organization or individual trying to discover his unique value and attempting to learn how to sell it.

Are you ready to learn to articulate your unique value? Then let's get started.

You Are the Value™

First, let me describe myself:

- I am just like you
- I am an entrepreneur
- I run my own long-term, quality growth business
- I have issues that keep me awake at night
- I face numerous issues to maintain and grow my client base
- I am challenged in my efforts to develop new business relationships
- I try to visualize the life I want, and I am continuing to build a compelling business model to attain that goal
- I realize the business has become more commoditized and that I need to distinguish myself in the marketplace
- I need to know my own value so that I can price it, sell it, and establish lifetime relationships based on this value with my core clients
- **I help other financial entrepreneurs with these same issues**

As you can see, I have many of the same challenges, concerns, frustrations and problems as you. The opportunities, needs and circumstances in my business and personal lives affect the achievement of my goals. I knew I had to go through an introspective process of knowing and discovering who I was before I could properly price my value, then learn how to sell that value more effectively to my targeted marketplace. Sound familiar?

I knew in order to achieve my goals that my single, most compelling challenge was to be world-class in the understanding of my own value. I knew the most important thing I could ever sell was ME. And the most important thing for you to sell is YOU! Neither one of us can afford to wing it.

The Value Revolution

As an FE, the single most compelling word in your vocabulary should be 'value.' This small, five-letter word is something we all have to get our hands around. Yes, I know the word is overused. Most people can't even define it. It means different things to different people. It's like asking you to define success. You get the picture. I will properly bring this word to life and help you understand it and appreciate it in ways you may not have considered.

Twenty years ago, the U.S. experienced a quality revolution. But in the late '80s and early '90s a new generation of quality was introduced: One that revolved around value. Who helped spearhead the new generation? Our clients. They were saying, "I have more options now, and you'd better be darned good at what you do if you want my business" Value became the single most compelling word in our sales vocabularies.

Think about the challenges your prospects and clients present to you. They may say or think, "What do you bring to the table?" and, "What can I expect from our working relationship?" or, "What is your value?"

Mack Hanan says in his book that instead of sitting across the table from your major clients, you should sit side-by-side, the way partners do. And to accomplish this, you need to be competitively advantaged. Says Hanan, "This strategy for selling is based on three prerequisites:

• You must know your value,
• You must price your value,
• You must sell your value."

He goes on to say, "If your clients do not know your value, they cannot perceive it. They will end up taking it from you. The best clients are those who cannot afford to do without your value." If you believe you truly are the value, and want to learn how to articulate it with confidence, passion and speed, read on. I will help you. I will teach you all about the Value Ladder–the unique seven-step process of discovering your value–and help you answer all the questions clients will ask (or are thinking about), in one way or another.

Competing on Value

To get to the essence of this theme of value, let's first talk about change. One of the elements of competing on value is being fully cognizant of change: How your clients are changing, how the marketplace is changing, how you are changing, and how these two short words–value and change–intersect with each other.

By integrating these themes in their books, authors like Robert Tucker, Mack Hanan, and Adrian Slywotzky have been able to pinpoint how value and change are revolutionizing the way we do business today. We need to truly understand how value and change affects our industry and, most importantly, our clients. We need to be introspective and to properly determine what is our value.

Here is a provocative passage from an article I quote in my training sessions. It embodies change and value and how to capture the opportunities they present:

"Companies often face changing markets, but few know how to exploit them. Many companies respond incrementally and passively as events unfold. Some even resist the arrival of a new reality. To profit from change, rather than be its victim, companies must use those trends to unlock value. The key is not to focus on projecting the trend itself, as many managers tend to do, but to assess how the trend will change the value a company is able to deliver to customers." (From, "Trend to Quantum Leap," *Financial Times*, Renee Mauborgne with Chan Kim)

So what are the trends impacting your business? Think of all the changes in your markets. Are you exploiting them? Are you resisting new realities in your business? Are you responding incrementally and passively? Are you profiting from change, or are you a victim? Are you unlocking your value?

You see, the single, most compelling thing you represent in the sales process is YOURSELF. You know it. I know it. Your clients and prospects know it. As good as your company's reputation is, as good as their million-dollar branding is, it's ultimately you who must stand out in the crowd. You are the one in front of that potential client answering their critical questions, and you are the one who compels the prospect either to do business with you or not. YOU are the value, my friend.

Whenever you communicate with a prospect or client, you are the team or organization. You can make it or break it. Always keep that in mind. Anyone in your organization who touches the prospect in one way or another needs to constantly reinforce this theme.

But I need your dedication and your belief that you can (and will) differentiate yourself from your competition by going through an intense process of introspection. Imagine you have a zipper on your chest. We will have to take that zipper down and open up your chest so we can reach in and pull out the answers. It might be painful, it might be difficult, but you cannot effect change until you know who you are. If you don't know your value, you can't sell it.

You know that serious business–building does not happen overnight. While reading motivational books, attending the pep club-type seminars, and trying various marketing approaches are an important part of your growth, these tools may not cause permanent change. The Value Ladder will provide the opportunity for the quiet introspection needed to effect true change in your life and your business.

If you are reading this book, it goes without saying that you are a dedicated and seriously committed FE, but are looking to improve. You're not satisfied with just being good, right? You want to elevate yourself from good…to great…to extraordinary! Do you want to make the leap to being extraordinary, but don't have a process? Do you want to be black-belt or top-gun in your approach?

Industry superstars who have achieved extraordinary status possess superior knowledge about their company, their solutions, their competitors, their business environment and marketplace. They know the issues, the problems, and they have solutions. They are problem solvers. They utilize the three critical ingredients of confidence, passion and speed in their sales presentations, while listening to critical questions prospects ask and answering with utmost respect. These individuals are your models to emulate.

As I mentioned at the beginning of this chapter, I wrestle with the same issues as you; they keep me awake at night. I believe I have empathy in talking to you as fellow entrepreneurs. In his popular book for entrepreneurs, *The E-Myth Revisited*, Michael Gerber says, "Most entrepreneurs are so busy working *in* their business, they are not spending enough time working *on* their business."

The Value Ladder process will help you work on your business, on your career, and on your personal life. That's why I also believe the Value Ladder and its unique process of discovery is more than a set of sales skills: they are life skills. I know FEs who have changed the direction of their careers as a result of the introspection process. Clients have told us that the Value Ladder has helped them focus on who they are, and what they do or do not want to do.

Are You in it For the Long Haul?

If you are, then you need to take a long, hard look at yourself in your mirror of introspection. You already know what plagues us all, we've talked about it: How to differentiate ourselves in a crowded marketplace. After years of studying sales behavior, and being in the industry trenches myself, I realized that the difficulty lies in identifying our own unique value. But once you master it, you realize: YOU ARE THE VALUE. This is a concept that can be understood well before you develop your own value. You are the value means just that–that you, not your product or your company, are the value.

$$\Bigg(\quad \text{Now, let's learn about the Value Ladder.} \quad \Bigg)$$

mirror mirror on the wall

am **i** the most valued

of them all?

CHAPTER TWO

Creation of the Value Ladder™

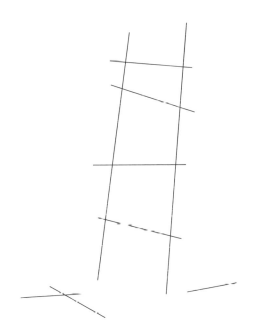

Creation of the Value Ladder™

The Tough Prospect Says:

"I don't know who you are.
I don't know your company.
I don't know what your company stands for.
I don't know your company's customers.
I don't know your company's products.
I don't know your company's reputation.
Now–what was it you wanted to sell me?"

– Harvey Mackay, *Swim with the Sharks*

Think of some of the sales dialogues you've had over the years. Can you recall some of the successful interactions you've experienced with clients and prospects? I can.

"Peter, I invested an entire day to properly prepare for the one hour you are giving me today." Those were my words to begin a meeting with the president of an organization I wanted to do business with. I could feel his appreciation in knowing I wasn't there to waste his time or mine. I researched his organization, spoke to his key employees–I knew the issues that were 'sitting on his desk'. Equally as important, I was prepared to answer his questions.

The scenario unfolded somewhat like Clint Eastwood's classic line in the movie, *Dirty Harry*, "Go ahead, make my day." Well I wasn't saying it, but I was thinking it: Ask me about my background, my value, my business beliefs, my process, client success stories, my differentiation, my potential, and my real value.

Go ahead, Peter, make my day.

Consider your own successful sales interactions. Do you remember:

• High-five feelings of accomplishment?
• Accolades from your management team?
• Trips and awards you've earned?
• Nice feelings rekindled?

How about the opportunities you've lost? Different feeling, huh? You get that knot in the pit of your stomach, and it's uncomfortable. If you've done everything possible to win, and still lose, you at least can look yourself in the mirror and know that you gave it your best shot. The common denominator in all of these scenarios is: A sophisticated, more informed, competitively enlightened prospect trying to obtain answers to his or her questions so he or she can decide whether or not to work with you.

Remember what I mentioned in the introduction, that the best way to learn how to sell is to first understand what it's like to buy? Think of the logical questions you might ask before making an important buying decision for your company, or for you and your family. Common sense tells you that you want to know more about the individual or the company you are considering. You want to know more about what they do. For example:

• Is their background impressive?
• Do they specialize in what you are looking for?
• Why are they doing this?
• What drives their thinking?
• Is their story compelling?
• Can you feel their passion?
• If you decide to work with them, what is their process?
• Who else have they done this for?
• Can you call somebody for a testimonial?
• What success have they had?

Do you feel more comfortable as you hear their answers? As your conversation deepens, especially if you're shopping around, you may want to know what makes them different. "I want to know more about your company," you may say. "I want to know more about your products/services/solutions. How are they different from your competitors? And, oh, by the way, I may want to know more about you as an individual. What do you stand for? What can I expect from working with you? And why should I make this decision to do business with you? What is the real value?"

If you are like me, you want to make a confident decision about someone *who is confident* with you. Throw in some passion and lack hesitation in responding to all of these buying thoughts and you've got the making of what we affectionately call the Value Ladder™.

How It All Began

What, exactly, is the Value Ladder™, anyway? It is the core component of a strategic development initiative that helps you begin the discovery process of differentiating your value from the competition. The Value Ladder is a process consisting of seven strategic steps (critical questions prospects usually ask or might be thinking) that prompt you to be introspective, ultimately helping you deliver your message with confidence, passion and speed (lack of hesitation).

It sounds simple and logical. And it is. That's the power of the model: It's simple and it's liberating. You can reply to most prospects' questions with one of the seven answers. Developing your seven answers will arm you for any situation.

But developing the Value Ladder wasn't so simple in the beginning. Let me tell you my story:

I began earning what I call my "on-the-job doctorate" in selling during my early years with the former Xerox Learning Systems.

During this period, I anguished over the questions: "How do I differentiate myself from the competition? What is my value? My process? How do I consistently articulate all of that to a prospect?" I knew if I wanted to make an impression on the financial services community and be able to train, coach, and enlighten financial entrepreneurs, I needed to relate to them, and deliver my unique value to them. That was my challenge. One of my early influences was sales trainer and author, Mack Hanan, and his book, *Competing on Value* that I mentioned in the introduction. I studied his concept of, "Before you can sell your value you have to know it." It made a lot of sense to me. After more research and some early practical applications, I decided to develop a value process for myself and my own business...a process that I later began teaching to others.

So, when I actually started creating the Value Ladder, I decided to go off-site for a strategic workshop with two members of my team to brainstorm and role-play. Where do I even begin, I thought?

Taking the First Step

Ok, I needed a starting point, so I thought, "What is the most logical question people ask when they first meet someone new? It's, "Hi, what's your name?" or, "Tell me a little bit about yourself." How many times can you remember meeting someone and after all of the "What's your name?" or "Who are you?" type questions, the next one usually was "What do you do?" Most people say, for example, "I'm a stockbroker," or "I'm with Merrill Lynch." But I always tell people who answer this way, "No, I know who you ARE, but what do you actually DO?" Sometimes they confuse who they are with what they do because in today's society you ARE what you do.

But being able to concisely answer the question, "Who Are You?" in a way that is compelling and differentiating will make an immediate impression on your prospect and go a long way toward making the first good emotional connection. It's also important to remember that it's the WAY you respond to the question that is important.

So just who are you? Well, we'll get into the nuts-and-bolts of who you are and how to articulate this a little later in the book; but, basically, it's your mission to give your prospect a tight definition of your organization/business/practice background with as much passion as you can muster. Your response must set the stage for the prospect to go to the next question, or step on the Value Ladder, "What Do You Do?"

The Next Logical Steps

So, as I continued to role-play with my team during the workshop, I realized that the second step on the Value Ladder, "What do you do?" became the early prompt to answering the Unique Value Proposition (UVP). The UVP is the single, most important statement capturing the essence of what you do that sets you apart from your competition.

As I moved through the process of developing the Value Ladder, it dawned on me that as we dissected and expanded the first two questions, we were unconsciously jumping to the eventual fourth question, which was, "How Do You Do What You Do?" and I realized that something was missing. *A step was definitely missing.* I noticed that in my role-playing, I would automatically answer the following question—the next logical step—"Why Do You Do What You Do?"

This question is very important because people want a quick story of "why," even though they may not pose the question in quite that way. What they want to know, in essence, are your core business beliefs. They want to know what makes you or your organization tick. They want to know what motivates you and what compels you to be in this business. This is where your story comes alive.

Thus the next logical point on the Value Ladder then became

the "Why" portion, which we immediately included in the seven critical questions.

Next, we developed the question, "How Do You Do What You Do?" This is the fourth step. A prospect might ask, for example, "How would you work with someone like me or my company?" or, "Can you explain your process?" This is where you position and illustrate your process in such a way that conveys you are a black-belt FE. I'll illustrate in detail a little later how this step on the Value Ladder works so beautifully.

So, as you continue walking up the Value Ladder (as we did in our own development process), you begin to understand how the questions–and your answers–become a finely tuned process. If you are talking to a prospect and you get to this point on the Value Ladder, the prospect usually will ask the next question, "Who Have You Done it For?" Or more to the point, "Who else do you work with? Could I be a client?" They will want to know about the successes you've had, and who are some of your typical clients. "Have you helped others? Am I the type of person you could help?"

Next, your prospect will want to know, "What Makes You Different?" This is the sixth step on the Value Ladder. You will be able to distinguish yourself on three levels: Your organization, your solutions and yourself. Here's where the theme of differentiation starts to come alive. As I explain fully in an upcoming chapter, your prospects may be interviewing a number of competitive alternatives, and you will need to know how to properly distinguish yourself from them.

Ultimately, your response to this question will help prospects and clients understand the depth and breadth of your differentiation, and establish you as being world-class.

The seventh and last question is "Why Should I Do Business With You?" Here, a prospect is saying to you, "What's your real value to me, and what am I going to get out of this partnership?" My belief is that business becomes a meeting of the hearts first, and then business becomes a meeting of the minds. Real value may be measured qualitatively or quantitatively. If you meet both the emotional and the intellectual needs of your clients, you are providing real value. Here you differentiate yourself by connecting with the prospect, on both an emotional and intellectual basis.

Why Didn't I Think of This Sooner?

In essence, the evolution of the seven questions came about as a common sense way of articulating my own introduction, my message, and my call to action to prospective clients. I'm proud to pass them on to you. You'll see, they work beautifully!

In reality, the Value Ladder simply helps the normal flow of conversation. By having all seven questions down pat, you'll further refine the critical answers to what is your value and how you differentiate yourself from competition. By my standard, answering all seven questions embodies the complete message of what your broad-based value is and how you come across to people. Prospects get a sense of the totality of who you are and what you represent.

But, I must tell you that discovering and delivering your value is a strategic process. It's what I refer to as a chess game of questioning, answering, and understanding. As an introspective process of discovery, the Value Ladder Process allows you to understand the seven critical questions clients ask, and to answer them with confidence, passion and speed.

You will learn how to be flexible, in the moment, in control, and quick on your feet during your sales presentations. And you will also learn how to meet the needs of your prospects while answering those seven critical questions. Plus, you can immediately implement these skills as you learn them.

The Value Ladder can also be viewed as your "virtual file cabinet." What do I mean? Read on to understand the simplicity of this model and its similarities to the many files and filing drawer cabinets in your office. The biggest difference is that this virtual file cabinet will eventually become the most important one in your office.

The Virtual File Cabinet™–Custom Answers in a Drawer

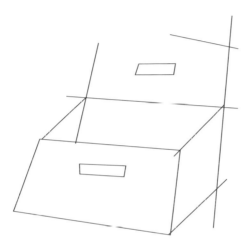

Think of the Value Ladder as your very own custom seven-drawer file cabinet–like an invisible file cabinet. To better understand this concept, visualize the file cabinets you have in your office. You probably have your files organized like this: Client files, competitor files, marketing files, financial information files, and so on. Most likely, contained in these files are similar manila folders, separating your important information. I'll help you build your virtual file cabinet as we go through the book, but first here's a preview of how it works:

Simply stated, each drawer in your virtual file cabinet equals one question on the Value Ladder. Visualize the seven drawers labeled with the names of the seven questions. In each drawer are your virtual manila folders containing the many ways you can answer each question. For example, if your first drawer is labeled, "Who Are You?" then you will have folders in that drawer labeled, "Business Background," and "Personal Background," both with as little or as much information as you may need to rely on at the appropriate moments of a client presentation, and so on for the remaining six questions.

As you continue to climb the Value Ladder, you'll have to think about your answers to each question as though you were building or creating your own virtual file cabinet. (I'll provide examples for you in each chapter.) You need to take this file cabinet with you everywhere—from prospect meetings to client meetings; from charitable events to social gatherings; from golf outings to elevators; from trains to plane trips—you never know when a question might pop up. Trust me, though, questions will come up in one way, shape or form…everywhere.

In Chapter 11, you'll also find six powerful applications for the virtual file cabinet to help you further deliver your message with passion, confidence and speed.

$\Big($ Now, it's time to start climbing the Value Ladder! $\Big)$

The Value Ladder™

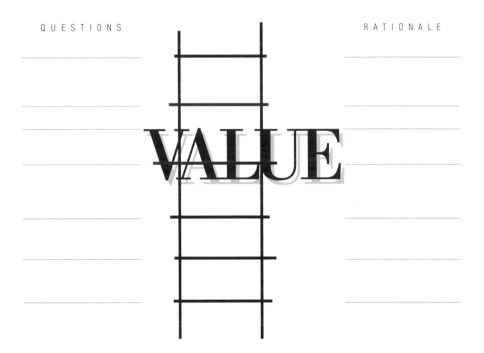

QUESTIONS

RATIONALE

T h e   V a l u e   L a d d e r™

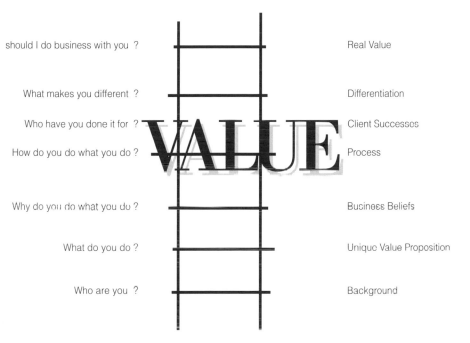

should I do business with you ?	Real Value
What makes you different ?	Differentiation
Who have you done it for ?	Client Successes
How do you do what you do ?	Process
Why do you do what you do ?	Business Beliefs
What do you do ?	Unique Value Proposition
Who are you ?	Background

mirror mirror on the wall
am **i** the most <u>valued</u>
of them all?

CHAPTER THREE

Who Are You?

Who Are You?

I woke up in a Soho doorway
The policeman knew my name

He said, "You can go sleep at home tonight
if you can get up and walk away."

I staggered back to the underground,
the breeze blew back my hair
I remembered throwing punches around
and preachin' from my chair.

> *Who are you*
> *Hu hu hu hu*
> *Who are you*
> *Hu hu hu hu*

– The Who

AF11640693. This was my brother Vince's serial number. He was in the Air Force Security Service Unit in Pakistan during the Vietnam War. I was about 10 years old. It's been over 30 years and I can still remember that identification number as though it were yesterday; it made such an impression on me.

AF11640693. There was something tangible about the ID. It was who he *was*. It was his name, rank and serial number. It identified him immediately. It was concise, and it was repeated over and again–the same ID. His serial number became the totality of who he was.

First impressions are so critical and we only get them once. We all have a "name, rank and serial number" in life. Can we say who we are as quickly and as consistently as those in the military are trained to do?

Who Are You?...three words that sound simple, and ask a simple question. But is it really? This is the first critical question that begins your journey up the Value Ladder. You'll need to stay on this bottom rung for a while, though, until your answers to this question are so engaging that your prospect will genuinely want to know more about you. If they don't ask, that means you haven't properly set the stage, and that you'll quickly lose their attention.

When someone asks about your background, how do you respond? With your name, rank and serial number? As I pointed out earlier, most often people want to know *what you do*, and not just your name and title as the question implies. And more often than not, this simple question is asked in many different ways.

For example, how many times has someone said to you, "Tell me a little bit about yourself," or, "Tell me more about your background." Or they may say, "How long have you been in the business," or perhaps, "Tell me more about your business experiences," and, more personally, "How long have you lived in this area?" If they aren't asking these types of questions, they are probably wondering about them.

It's important to have answers to this question in all of the different ways people will ask you it. This is when you can literally pull out the appropriate answer from your "file drawer" in your virtual file cabinet so it's easier for you to deliver the appropriate response.

As you read through this chapter you'll learn how to establish immediate credibility with your prospect and how to articulate your organization/business/practice background and, if and when appropriate, your personal background. *I repeat: If and when appropriate.*

But, first, let me tell you a story that really got me thinking about "who we really are," and the types of things that make a lasting impression.

First... and Lasting Impressions

When you answer the question, "Who Are You?" and identify yourself in a confident and passionate way, allowing the other person to *feel* who you really are, you make a powerful emotional connection that results in a lasting impression. That's why it's so important to have a consistent response to all of these questions, because it sets the stage for your continuing discussion with the prospect.

"Who Are You?" is, quite literally, the first question out of the gate. And what you don't want to do is to wing it right off the bat. Some might call it "dancing" around the subject, which is a kissing cousin to winging it. Others might call it beating around the bush. No matter what you call it, it's all just hesitation and an obvious lack of confidence in yourself and your message.

Think about how powerful it is to look eyeball to eyeball at a prospect when they say, "Tell me about yourself" and deliver a precise answer. What are the five top answers that you would give a prospect to introduce yourself and your organization? Do you immediately know what you would say–without any hesitation?

What would you say if David Letterman, Oprah or Ted Koppel put a microphone in your face on TV and asked, "Who are you?" Could you answer without stuttering and stammering? Could you answer with confidence, passion and speed? Could you be precise, without gulping and searching for words, without dancing or winging it?

Use Your Intuition

Your answers should prompt further questions from prospects. Remember, you always should be in the moment and flexible with your responses. Here's an example of what I typically say when I'm asked "Who Are You"-type questions:

"I'm Leo Pusateri, the president of Pusateri Consulting and Training. We are a sales consulting and training organization headquartered in <u>beautiful</u> Buffalo, New York and we <u>specialize</u> and <u>partner</u> with financial service organizations and financial entrepreneurs to help them compete more effectively on the philosophies of value." The key words I've underlined have special meaning and are ones I consistently use in my message. My clients might laugh when I talk about *beautiful* Buffalo, but they remember it–and me. The same goes for the words *specialize* and *partner* which mean I teach clients and special friends I affectionately call financial entrepreneurs.

A person might say, "Well, Leo, how long have you been doing this?" or they might say, "Tell me more about your background." So you see, even though they begin by asking who I am, many times they will ask more questions and go deeper wanting to know more about me both personally and professionally.

I always tell FEs that it's not necessary to share all of the information at once. Use your common sense and intuition and only share information about yourself if it is appropriate. The key word here is *appropriate.*

Your intuition will always tell you how much is enough. You don't need to be a motor-mouth. You don't need to say, "Let me tell you *everything* about my business and personal background." This might not be the appropriate time to talk about such things as civic activities, family, education, and special interests. It all depends on the emotional connection you're making at the time. You have to be in the moment with each prospect or client. In each client situation, you have to intu-itively assess how much is appropriate. Experience will make it easier for you over time.

Think about how you would respond to the "Who Are You?" question. Does your response position you in important ways? Is your response helping create further dialogue and trust? Is it building rapport with your client?

It's very important to remember as you prepare to explain who you are, that the *way in which you respond* makes that critical first impression. You know the adage: You don't get a second chance to make a first impression. We all know that's true.

How Do You Rate?

I held a broker meeting at a wirehouse where several million-dollar producers were in the audience. I decided to conduct the confidence meter exercise discussed earlier in the introduction. I asked the audience, "On a confidence continuum, on a scale of 1-10, how would you rate yourself? Number one on the scale would be, 'No Confidence.' The fifth level might be, 'I'm some-what confident, but I need help.' And the highest level, number 10, would be, 'I'm Tiger Woods, Michael Jordan, Wayne Gretzky-get-out-of-my-face-I–can-answer-this-question-with-the-best-of-them.'"

Where do you feel you are on this confidence meter?"

As I went around the room, the participants (remember, many were million-dollar producers) were rating themselves at 8, 9, 10. Every now and then someone would rate themselves as a 3 or a 4, so I was prompted to ask, "You guys are very successful already. I'm curious, why would you rate yourself so low? Are you just being tough on yourself or what?" Several concurred,

"As successful as we are, it still is something that we take for granted. We wing it."

You need to get out of the gate with a powerful start. If you don't, your prospect may quickly tune you out way before the other six questions can be answered.

Are You Ready to Get Down to Work?

The Value Ladder concept takes off immediately with everyone you come in contact with. When you dialogue with them, they are forming impressions of you instantly. As you climb the Value Ladder and continue to trust the process, you'll return to the early questions such as, "Who Are You?" with even better perspective. I have seen individuals reach the sixth step on the Value Ladder, "What Makes You Different" and suddenly realize there are common themes running through all seven answers to the Value Ladder questions.

If you called 10 of your clients, and asked them to describe you, would the same themes run throughout their comments about you as might be running throughout your own Value Ladder answers? If you feel confident, self-assured, and knowledgeable–would your clients say the same things about you?

Find a quiet place where you can think about–and write down–the answers to the question, "Who Are You?" Here are some guidelines to follow.

- Say who you are by giving your name and title, then who you work for.

- Explain your organization. Provide the firm's history, strategic alliances, relationships and how long it has been in existence.

- If you're part of a team or a department, identify it.

- Describe its function and explain how your team or department operates, and what your role is.

If you feel it is appropriate, the following information can be presented to your client as well:

Professional Considerations

- Your location
- Years in business
- Years with current organization
- Members of your team
- Former employers
- Key clients
- New clients on annual basis
- Assets under management
- Areas of expertise
- Professional designations/special education
- Professional affiliations
- Special background
- Other considerations

Personal Considerations

- Where you live
- Where you grew up
- Family information
- Educational background
- Hobbies
- Sports you enjoy
- Other non-work activities
- Charities or civic organizations

I have found that many people take these considerations for granted. Those who personally reflect on the question, "Who are you?" will find the stage set for the introspection that continues with developing your UVP.

Your Very Own Quiz Show

Now that you've thoroughly examined who you are with thought-provoking questions, it's a good idea to test yourself on how well you could answer, "Who Are You?" in a real situation. Remember, you don't want to practice on your prospect. So practice now.

Here are some strategic questions to consider:

- How well do I position myself now?
- What is my typical response to the question, "Who Are You?"
- How does my response help to begin my differentiation process?
- How does my response help to set the stage for further dialogue, building trust and rapport?
- What other information does my team need to answer this question at a world-class level?
- If my team and I can answer this question at a world-class level, what impact will this have on the sales or consulting process?
- What impression will I make in the marketplace if my organization fails to respond to this question with confidence, passion and speed?

This is a good time to remind you that your virtual file cabinet comes into play here in very important ways. Remember, your first drawer is titled, "Who Are You?" and the first manila folder is labeled, "Business Background." You should have another one titled, "Personal Background," and both files will include information you can repeat frontward and backward about your message.

The beauty of the virtual file cabinet is that you can visualize the key points you need to make, and *virtually pull from your resources* the material you need to make your presentation more powerful and compelling.

A Case in Point

I was asked to conduct a Value Ladder workshop for executives of two firms who were finalizing a strategic partnership. It was a potentially exciting venture bringing together two leading-edge firms. However, they couldn't agree how their combined salesforces should position this new endeavor. We addressed our Value Ladder questions with similar frustrations. It didn't surprise me to hear that the proposed partnership was never finalized.

The introspection beginning with "Who Are You?" is strategic discovery at its best. Don't take this question for granted. It's like blocking and tackling in football, basic but critical. Adherence to discipline and mastery will set you apart. It starts with the first Value Ladder question. If you can't settle on an answer to "Who Are You?" then you might as well forget about trying to answer the remaining questions.

Don't Be Afraid to Look Yourself in the Eye

Look in your mirror. Spend some time reflecting. "Who Are You?" is an easy question to answer on the surface. But with proper introspection and reflection you soon realize how deep your self-analysis can go. You'll be surprised at what you'll learn about yourself by going through this exercise. You'll reveal aspects of yourself that you previously didn't think of bringing up, even to your existing clients.

Discovery starts with that first step and, in turn, will give you ammunition to make a powerful first impression. It's much like reading a good book. To keep you turning the pages, a book must capture your interest or curiosity immediately. But it also must continue to keep your interest throughout, all the way to a dynamic and satisfying end.

One of the most important lessons you can take with you after reading this chapter is this:

A compelling response to the question "Who Are You?" will automatically lead your prospect to ask, "What Do You Do?" – the next question on the Value Ladder. If your answer to this first question is thought-provoking enough to lead the prospect to ask you, "Well, what do you do?" then you have crafted and perfected the answer to the first step on the Value Ladder.

Each Value Ladder question, in essence, acts as a springboard for the next one.

No matter how good you think your answers are, there still are more opportunities to make them even tighter. Use your virtual screwdriver. If you want to go from good...to great...to extraordinary, it will require ongoing alignment of all your answers to ensure the perfect response. Keep an open mind and keep your screwdriver handy as you go through all the questions on the Value Ladder.

Now, you should be prepared for the second step, "What Do You Do?" and the development and creation of your Unique Value Proposition (UVP).

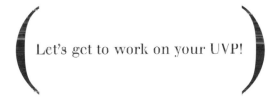

Let's get to work on your UVP!

mirror mirror on the wall

am **i** the most valued

of them all?

CHAPTER FOUR

What Do You Do?

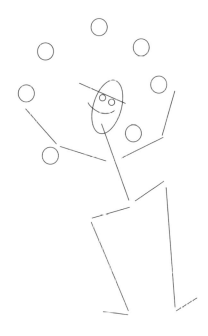

What Do You Do?

*Vain attempts to imitate others no
longer will I make.
Instead I will place my uniqueness on
display in the marketplace.
I will proclaim it, yea, I will sell it.*

– Og Mandino,
The Greatest Secret in the World

"So, what do you do, Dad?"

I can still remember the dialogue with my oldest child, Leighann. She was eight at the time, the age when questions are fired at rapid pace. You've probably been there before–when someone's inquisitiveness takes them on a path of discovery. The answer to one question leads to more questions.

It's an FBI-type interrogation at its best. But, in this case, the intent is purely innocent. The questions are so simple and represent a genuine sense of really wanting to understand.

"I teach people how to sell, Leighann."

"What do you mean, Dad?"

It sounded like I gave her a good, succinct answer. What seemed so simple to me was still so confusing to her.

"Well, honey, can you think of anything that Mom has bought for you recently?"

"What do you mean, 'bought for me?'"

Are you starting to get a sense of this probing specialist I had created? On one hand, I was trying to be patient with her. On the other hand, I was smiling within as I witnessed her "professional" persistence. She wasn't satisfied yet. I still had not answered her question.

"How about a toy or a dress or maybe those roller skates you have in the garage?" I said.

"Okay, Dad, but I still don't know what you mean," Leighann responded.

Isn't it amazing that as the world becomes more and more complex, the challenge for simplicity in our work and in our dialogue is becomes more and more valued? How could I, in simple conversation with my daughter, speak to her at her level of understanding? How could I explain this in layman terms?

"Well, Leighann, you know when you go to the mall with Mom and Dad and we stop at a store to buy something we need? It may be something for you or your sisters, or something for the house. Isn't there usually someone working there who is trying to help us with what we are looking for?"

"Yes, Daddy."

My instincts confirmed that I was on to something.

"And, Leighann, can you think of what those people do?"

"Well, they ask if they can help you."

"What else, honey?"

"They ask you questions about what you are looking for. They help you look for things. They answer your questions, and–oh yeah, Dad, they ask if there is anything else you need."

"You've got it, Leighann. I help those kinds of people talk to other people in a better way. Sometimes, a nicer way. I help them with the questions they ask and how to respond to the answers we give them. I really help them to feel good about what they do so that other people will feel good about it, too."

"That's selling, Dad?"

"That's selling, Leighann."

Sometimes, explaining to a child what you do can unravel all of the mystery and complication of trying to articulate your value, by forcing you to put your definition in clear and simple terms.

Defining Your Unique Value Proposition™ (UVP™)

The second step on the Value Ladder, "What Do You Do?" helps you develop your unique value proposition. This is what your prospect really wants to know. So what, exactly, is your Unique Value Proposition (UVP)? It is a brief statement or paragraph that clearly and concisely captures the essence of what differentiates you from your competition. It is your compelling message delivered with such confidence, passion and speed that you will really feel on top of your game.

You know the great feeling when someone looks you in the eye, is unbelievably conversationally proficient, speaks with respect, is precise with her words, and customizes and personalizes her dialogue to you at such a high level. Well, doesn't that make an incredible impression on you? Don't you feel like you're dealing with someone who is the consummate professional? Someone who is on top of her own game, and has invested time, energy, and money getting her story, the unique branding of her practice and/or her team down. You can feel the black-belt aura of that person, right?

You leave with the feeling that person connected with you, that she asked the right questions, and she had her act together. Wouldn't you like your prospects and clients to feel this way about you?

Of course you would!

As we begin to outline the step-by-step process of creating your own UVP, it will become clearer to you just how important and critical it is to capture the attention of your prospect. Your UVP is a powerful statement. It's not just the exercise of introspection and discovering and developing it that are important, but also learning how to articulate it with confidence, passion and speed.

It's easy to create a confident, succinct statement. Let's break down the individual words (unique-value-proposition) to get a clearer picture:

- **Unique:** You are one of a kind; or as I say, you have exclusivity
- **Value:** How well your solutions help achieve your client's goals
- **Proposition:** Your written or verbal proposal

In essence, your UVP is your proposal of what you feel you do so uniquely well in providing your value to others.

Your UVP sets the stage for your differentiation, and should imply to your prospects that what you do is special. It should generate interest, and give a definite sense of your expertise. It also should open the door of opportunity for people to say, "Tell me more about what you do," or "What do you mean by that?"

A UVP is not a tag line, a slogan, a logo, or corporate mission statement. It should, however, include your specialization and tell your prospects and clients about your world-class business. A branding phrase such as Nike's "Just Do It" is a great advertising slogan, but is not a UVP. Your UVP is longer than a tag line, but not as comprehensive as a mission statement–it's the best of both in a few sentences. Other close relatives to the UVP are positioning statements, vision statements, and selling propositions.

In previous chapters you've learned that discovering your value is an introspective process. It takes deep thought and introspection and is a process of many drafts, not just simply jotting down notes on a sheet of paper. As you continue through this chapter, I'll give you examples of UVPs and step-by-step guidelines to help you create your own.

If your organization already has its own UVP, you should determine if it's appropriate to use as is, or if it needs refining. Usually a single UVP for a financial services firm is all that's needed; everyone should be "singing from the same hymnal."

For example, my client, San Diego-based money manager Nicholas-Applegate Capital Management, used our process to develop a UVP for their wrap fee partners. Their sales and marketing team presented it this way: **"We provide unique solutions to help you build and enhance your fee-based business."** So instead of just saying, "We manage money," they went deeper by mentioning things in their UVP that their clients would probably want to know more about. Unique solutions? Tell me more about them. Help me build a fee-based business. How? Help me enhance my existing fee based business. How?

I've seen a lot of organizations struggle to get consistent answers from their sales force regarding their UVP. Nicholas-Applegate has invested considerable time and dollars to create a world-class sales organization. They should be applauded for their commitment.

Focus on Your Marketplace

When you really think about your business strategies, the types of people you want to work with, and the kind of professional and personal life you're trying to create for yourself, you find it's that much easier to focus on what you truly do. That's what happened to me when I decided to focus on the financial services area. I realized in my own career that the more I increased my focus, the more I knew where my uniqueness and my positioning should be in this world.

Once you determine your own uniqueness, it's fairly simple to create your UVP and answer all of the critical questions asked by your clients. My UVP says it simply: **We empower organizations and individuals to discover and articulate their unique value.** Here's the real key: It's so much easier to answer the question, "What Do You Do?" when you speak from your heart and your soul. You'll find you exude more confidence about your special gifts and talents.

Speaking in the Real World

Here's the real test of effectiveness. You must create a statement you can use both in business and personal situations. This does not mean you should repeat the exact verbiage word-for-word. What it does mean is that now you have the basic foundation for the question, "What Do You Do?" which will allow you to customize your statement to the situation, or the person. That's when you should go into your virtual file cabinet, pull out the appropriate response, and make it come alive with your confidence, passion and speed.

For example, if you met someone on the golf course and they asked you "What do you do?" you probably wouldn't be robotic and recite your exact written UVP. No, you would be conversational and friendly, of course. However, most of what you would deliver would be taken from your basic message, which should be consistent time after time.

Now after you've delivered your answer to this person on the golf course, how would you want him to describe you to someone else? Think about this for a moment. What type of message can you deliver in 10 seconds? Did you create an aura that would lead this person to say to his spouse, friend or colleague that you were really impressive?

Here's something else to consider: If you are on a plane making polite conversation, and the person next to you asks, "What do you do?" remember they are, in effect, asking you the second question on the Value Ladder. They might say, "Hi, my name is Joe. What's yours? What do you do?" It's unlikely this person would ask, "Hi, who are you?" in quite that way. They won't ask you about your background directly, instead they simply say, "What do you do?"

After you reply with your name and what you do, you can extend your description to include your entire UVP. Again, make it come alive by personalizing it while you are in the moment with that person. That's when you become black-belt or top-gun in the delivery of your unique value proposition.

Here's what happened when FE Kathy Peer took a cross-country flight recently. Kathy is a partner with The Private Consulting Group, a national wealth management firm. She is based in the Albany, New York area and her firm specializes in wealth optimization. She works with affluent investors on estate planning and legacy issues, among other things. Kathy was one of the participants in a three-hour training program I held, and seemed to really connect with the message. As a black-belt in this industry, she is polished, committed and expert as evidenced by a family worth $50 million she recently contracted with.

Her organization had created a very expensive, beautiful color brochure that she was very proud of. But one afternoon she called me and said, "Leo, I just spent a lot of money on my new brochure, explaining what I do. Recently thereafter I was flying first-class and sitting next to a person who asked me "What do you do?" And as the gentleman asked me this question, I was really caught off guard. I wondered how I could net my answer out to this person? As it turned out, he was a senior executive affiliated with a major sports organization. He had access to tons of people, he was very influential, and it really hit me how critical it was to get the answers out in a consistent fashion so that I would not be winging it, and lose a prospect right out the gate."

She went on to say, "It amazes me to think of the dollars we've invested in our branding, and of all the success we've had. And yet it is still so difficult and challenging to clearly answer the simple, basic questions regarding our distinction, and to be able to express it with confidence, passion, and speed."

We've all been in this type of situation before. There are many ways to respond to the question, but instead of saying *exactly* what is stated on your written UVP, you could instead say something more informal. For example, I might respond this way, "I'm Leo Pusateri, it's nice to meet you. I'm from the beautiful Buffalo area and I own my own sales consulting and training firm that specializes in the financial marketplace. I work with a lot of prestigious companies and individuals who are challenged to distinguish themselves."

If my intuition advised me, then I might add, "This is a crowded marketplace today. I help clients answer questions about what makes them different and why people should do business with them. I've developed a company that helps individuals and firms answer those questions at levels they have truly never thought about before."

And that whole statement takes about 15 seconds to deliver. I made my UVP come alive. Read it out loud and you'll see what I mean.

But if I told that same person, "Hi, my name is Leo Pusateri and I do sales training," do you think they would have an understanding of what I really do? What does "sales training" really mean, after all? It could mean anything. Many times, we don't know how to answer the question at the highest level of conversational proficiency. To be sure, sometimes the situation calls for the "short and dirty" version. That said, you must be careful not to answer *who you are* instead of what you do.

How To Develop Your UVP™

Let's get started developing your UVP. You may want to jot down a few things on paper.

The **first step** is to think about the various words that describe the unique value of your company. Here is a sample listing of words that typically come up:

- Minimizes risk
- Global
- Regional
- Specializes in wealth management
- Specialist
- Partner
- Industry innovator
- Socially responsible
- International provider
- Preserves capital
- Peerless customer service
- Seeks superior results
- Has competitive edge
- Rigorously implements strategy
- Market leader
- Alignment with clients
- Consistent track record
- Old-line heritage

If I gave you 60 seconds to brainstorm some ideas, what would the key words on your list be? Give it a try.

The **second step** is to consider the words that best describe the unique value of the solutions you provide. For example:

- Portfolio managers on the same side of table with analysts
- Managers have meetings with clients, if needed
- Multiple portfolio management systems
- Comprehensive
- Customized
- Personalized
- Large, but entrepreneurial
- Proven, unique process
- Analysts are money managers
- Broadly diversified
- Low volatility
- Capital market insights
- Institutional quality money management

Again, if I gave you another 60 seconds to brainstorm some ideas, what would the key words on your list be? Keep going. You've got some momentum now.

Third, think about all of the words that describe the unique value of YOU as an individual, such as:

- Skillful
- Proficient
- Experienced
- Capable
- Intelligent
- Clever
- Resourceful
- Compassionate
- Informed
- Trusted
- Expert
- Master
- Competent
- Prepared
- Sharp
- Methodical
- Trustworthy
- Aware
- Distinctive
- Understanding
- Smart
- Accomplished
- Efficient
- Talented
- Discreet
- Inventive
- Ethical
- Educated
- Sophisticated
- Honest

Take another 60 seconds to brainstorm some additional words to describe you. Is there anything else you would add to this list?

Now that you have a list of key words, your **fourth step** is to choose up to ten that really jump out at you. Use them as a starting point for the first draft of your UVP.

The **fifth step** is to begin writing your initial draft. When you are satisfied with the first version, review it carefully and make any changes you feel necessary. Have a colleague read it. Leave it for a few days, then go back to it with a fresh outlook. A final UVP comes together as you continue to go up the Value Ladder.

Why not ask for input from your most valuable resources–your current clients? To do so, send them a letter, or just pick up the phone and ask what they believe are some of your unique qualities. Better yet, visit them. Nothing is better than a face-to-face meeting to catch up on details, as well as to convey a thank-you for their business. It's also a nice time to get feedback from them regarding ways you can improve.

Other questions you might ask are: Why did you hire me? What were some of the key points that led you to work with me? What do you value the most in working with me? What is the real value I provide to you?

It's critical to keep a pulse of what's important to your clients so you can continue to provide the value that's vital to them. You need to be sensitive to your core marketplace. Plus, it helps you to continue refining your UVP as your clients change and as the marketplace evolves.

Here are a few guidelines as you begin writing your draft:

• Make your UVP one sentence or a brief statement
• Be specific
• Convey a positive, passionate and confident feeling

- Create an emotional connection through your words
- Have your statement create enough interest and excitement so that someone would say, "Tell me more about that."
- Write your UVP to fit on the back of your business card, if compliance permits

Be prepared to answer your prospect's follow-up questions, such as, "What do you mean by that?" or, "Tell more about that." You want to emphasize certain words in your sentences to make your message memorable. Be prepared to take the key words and/or phrases that you emphasize deeper. This will really help make your UVP come alive.

It's also important to edit and re-write because as you do, your UVP becomes more concise and clear. Continue reviewing your draft until your message conveys a positive, passionate and confident feeling to create an emotional connection when you deliver it.

It's not necessary to have more than one UVP, even if you serve different markets such as both pre- and post-retirees, widows, small business owners, physicians, etc. You are who you are, and you do what you do, regardless of your markets. The manila folders in your virtual file cabinet will help you customize your answers to questions germane to specific market segments, when the occasions arise.

To help spark your creativity, here are a few sample UVPs used by FEs:

I provide wealth management services that assist clients to reduce taxes, eliminate the fear of financial loss, and retire comfortably by meeting their financial goals.

I enable individuals to make more informed decisions about their money, the growth and protection of their assets, and providing estate planning solutions.

I offer customized investment strategies that are academically based and give clients the greatest chance of reaching their financial goals.

I offer comprehensive, objective financial advice to clients who desire a high level of personal service.

Your UVP™ Should be a Custom Fit

I was conducting a seminar recently and some of the participants in the group decided to test me. They asked, "Leo, what do you do?" and I said, "I work with financial consultants like yourselves, and I help them go through a discovery process of true introspection to learn what their unique value is. I also teach them how to articulate it with enhanced confidence, passion and speed."

Then I said, "Take a look at my Unique Value Proposition. It is, **Empowering financial organizations and financial entrepreneurs to discover and articulate their unique value.**"

I asked them, "Do you think I say that to everybody? Of course it's the only UVP that I have, but I can make it come alive in many different ways." I went on to explain how to customize the UVP for each prospect or client, and how to prevent it from sounding robotic, all the while delivering the message in a clear and consistent way.

Now, what if you had an appointment with a referral. Are you prepared to deliver a consistent answer to the question, "What Do You Do?" Is the answer similar to the one you gave the person on the plane, or on the golf course? Most likely not. You might be thinking, "Well, I really don't need to explain a lot about what I do since this prospect is a referral, and they already know what I do." But I say to you—do they really?

UVPs can not only impress prospects, but they also can reveal new assets from existing clients. Many clients may not understand the breadth of your services. Here is an example that illustrates the point:

A high-level FE working for an international client of mine did not realize the scope of what he offered his own clients. He calls on the Pacific Rim markets and his focus is high-tech and biomedical corporate executives. This FE told me a story about a client of his, relating that he verbalized his new UVP to the client during a meeting. When his client heard him discuss the integrated solutions he could offer, the client said, "I thought you just sold stocks and bonds. I didn't realize you offered these types of customized solutions." He thought the FE was just a stockbroker.

As a result, the FE was able to uncover hidden assets. His UVP also mentioned his work in liquidity strategies. And, after bringing in a product specialist, he opened a $2 million account, a direct result of having a newly developed UVP.

Clients may know you are a financial consultant or an FE, and they may know that others think highly enough of you to provide a referral. But, do they really know what your proposal of unique value is? Let's say you are now in a business setting. You most likely talked through the initial pleasantries. You've built rapport, and maybe you've both talked about your respective backgrounds. At the appropriate moment, you should then say, "Now, I'd like to spend a few minutes to walk you through my unique value proposition."

At this point, you would say something like, "I partner with businesses like yours (or families like yours). I establish and deliver a comprehensive financial planning process (or investment process) that will put us on the same side of the table. This will ensure the successful attainment of many of your long-term goals. And that's what I do."

You can see in the dialogue above how effective your UVP can be.

You can never spend too much time on discovering the answer to the question, "What Do You Do?" Learning how to articulate that answer with a unbelievable feeling of flexibility and being in the moment will give you much more inner confidence from knowing who you really are. By understanding what your unique value proposition is, it's a lot easier to say no to certain prospects (when necessary). When you are on task and "on purpose," you are delivering your unique value proposition to the marketplace you covet.

Stay on task for the type of business and the lifestyle you are trying to build. The process is based on the best introspection possible, evaluating the full uniqueness and the importance of the total package you are selling...YOU!

Strategic Questions to Consider

- Do you have a Unique Value Proposition?
- If yes:
  - Are you and your team able to articulate your UVP with confidence, passion, and speed?
  - Is it a clear and consistent statement, right for your market?
  - How was it developed?
  - Who was responsible for developing it?
  - What process did you use to develop it?
  - When was it developed and is it still appropriate?
- What is your typical response to the question, "What do you do?"
- Is this the desired response?
- To what degree can your team answer this question based on the desired response?
- Where is the UVP used?
- If you have no UVP, what other kissing cousins of the UVP do you or your organization have?
  - Tag line/label/slogan
  - Brand strategy
  - Selling proposition (or unique selling proposition)

- Mission statement/Vision statement
- Values statement

To support this compelling story even further, let's really explore what your business beliefs are.

Now, let's climb the next step on the Value Ladder.

mirror mirror on the wall
am **i** the most valued
of them all?

CHAPTER FIVE

Why Do You Do What You Do?

Why Do You Do What You Do?

I don't hit every fairway,
I don't sink every putt,
I don't birdie every hole,
I don't win every tournament,
but, I believe that I will.

– Tiger Woods

For two consecutive years, my family and I packed up our Chevy Venture to head for Williamsburg, Virginia for Easter vacation. Busch Gardens, Colonial Williamsburg–here we come! With our 9" portable TV/VCR, my wife and I were well-prepared to meet the entertainment needs of our four kids. One of the viewing pleasures for the kids, and a listening pleasure for me and my wife in the front seats (we obviously couldn't see the video) was the movie, "Space Jam." Its popular theme song, "I Believe I Can Fly" still rings in my ears today. This mix of animated and real-life adventure features basketball legend Michael Jordan who, I feel, really believed he could fly!

Well, what do YOU believe so strongly that other people will get goose bumps when watching you perform or from listening to your story? In other words, *why* do you do what you do?

Now that we're on the third step of the Value Ladder, you'll quickly learn that this critical question, "Why Do You Do What You Do?" begins to lay the foundation for the compelling story of your business. This foundation is comprised of your business beliefs. These beliefs are connective themes that express to a prospect what you are so passionate about.

Why?

Arguably the most thought-provoking word in the English language...the question, "Why?" It forces us to think deeply and answer with heartfelt conviction. You need to be ready to connect your answer to the many ways clients can pose this question, including, "Why do you feel so strongly about that?" or, "Why do you feel your approach is the best way to go?" or, "Why do you do things this way?"

Why we do what we do is very personal to us, and can be a tricky question to teach on the Value Ladder. Sometimes people jump the gun, and will answer, "Because I love my job, that's why," or, "Because I love helping people, and I care for my clients."

On the surface, this response sounds good. However, the answer to this question should be *why you sell what you sell*, not how you treat your clients. There's a big difference here: Why you do what you do should be reflected in your business beliefs. A kissing cousin of these beliefs are your philosophies, such as your investment philosophy, your financial planning philosophy, or your wealth management philosophy.

Business beliefs represent the compelling story of your business. They set the stage to further tighten your UVP, and they give your prospect an understanding of your philosophical beliefs and the framework for your thought processes.

I tell FEs in my program that, of course, I care about my clients. I treat people with respect and I have integrity. But that's not *why* I do what I do. That's what I *stand* for. Those are some of my standards. Those are some of my core values. Just because you are passionate or accountable–well, that doesn't tell me why you do what you do. It just tells me what you stand for, and what I can expect from working with you.

There are subtle but important differences in ways to answer this question. We'll discuss the distinctions in detail a little later. When you eventually distinguish these differences in your model, the answers become very powerful when delivered.

Do You Believe?

Like most of us, I remember doing crazy things in college. During that 1973-77 span in my life there was one national preacher whose famous phrase was, "Do you believe in Jesus?" If you channel surf on your TV today–and I must admit to this occassional habit of mine–you'll find numerous religious preachers and evangelists emphasizing what they believe with unbelievable passion and delivery to thousands of worshippers.

During a spring break trip to Florida, I used to do a good impression of that memorable preacher from my Daytona Beach hotel balcony to my college buddies below. I would shout the chant, "Do you BELIEVE?" over and over. That was one of our most fun moments, and I still laugh when I think about it.

But the question for you is…What do YOU believe?

Defining Business Beliefs

Your business beliefs can come out in different ways. Someone may want to know what your beliefs are regarding the stock market, or the philosophy surrounding your work. They may be your thoughts regarding investments, how you manage money, your financial planning philosophy, tax beliefs, protection perspectives and so on.

Think about sources for this answer from outside of your work-life. Sometimes it's easier to start there and come back to what you do every day in your profession. If you are married, what are some of the successful traits of a solid, happy, loving marriage? If you are a parent, what are the keys to developing great relationships with your kids? If you are involved in a worthy cause or support a local charity, what gets you so excited and passionate about seeking support from others? If you admire a team of any kind, what makes that team so successful? Consider the totality of your experiences. Perhaps you see traits in a school board on which you are a member, or maybe you've had a positive experience working with a world-class company.

You see things that make others successful so the big question comes back to you, "Why do you do what you do?" and "What are your business beliefs?" When you think about your answer to the *why* question, remember to focus on *why* you recommend certain strategies or approaches. Keep in mind, your business beliefs should relate to and support your UVP. A tight connection between your UVP and business beliefs will take your differentiation to a deeper level.

How are Your Business Beliefs Founded?

Business beliefs are based on four factors:

First, you need to take into account the direction in which your organization/practice is headed, which may include the investment climate and industry trends. Consider which industry trends are affecting your organization right now so you get a clear picture of how to structure your business beliefs for your UVP. For instance:

- Are you positioning integrated, seamless financial solutions versus selling products?
- Are you attempting to differentiate your process?
- Are you committed to developing a fee-based business?
- Are you focusing on gathering assets?
- Are you truly committed to competing on value?
- Are you consulting with clients, or are you still transacting?
- Are you perceived as a registered vendor, or the client's one-and-only consultant?

Let's say you are a transactional broker. What would your beliefs be? You research stocks that outperform, find good ideas and pass them on to your clients. If, on the other hand, you are an investment management consultant, your beliefs lie in the power of the comprehensive investment management process, the power of institutional money management, the power of committing to investment policy statements, and applying standards of due diligence and quarterly monitoring. You may find that particular elements of your process are also reflected in your core business beliefs.

Second, business beliefs also are founded on where your practice has been, which means looking at historical patterns:

- Do you earn your revenues on a commission basis?
- Do you regularly compete on price or value?
- Do you focus on transactions?
- Are you selling products and not emphasizing a consultative approach?

Third, what have you learned as an organization? What opinions, wisdom, and experience have you developed in your practice? What have your clients taught you?

- You know what you like/don't like
- You know what works best for you
- You know, more importantly, what works best for your clients
- You know that your clients have taught you many things over the years

Fourth, I've recently realized that, sadly, there is another way business beliefs can be formulated. I refer to them as unexpected events in your life or business. Following is a true story that truly impacted me and my belief system. As we all know, unexpected events can change our outlook, as well as our answers within seconds, minutes and hours.

No Time To Mourn

"Leo, I don't think you know that my wife passed away three weeks ago." Those were the words that my friend and client, Mark Colgan, greeted me with during a follow-up meeting to review his newly created brochure. I felt like someone had hit me with a two by four.

Mark is a 31-year-old financial advisor with McDonald Investments in their Rochester, New York office. Can you imagine Mark's pain and grief after suddenly losing his 28-year old wife, Joanne? They were married seven years before heart disease caused her death. What I saw and heard in Mark was true love, devotion and his coming to grips with an unexpected change in his life.

It was less than a year before that Mark had attended one of our "Discovering Your Value" retreats in Chicago. Mark was challenged at the time to get his unique story down. Relatively young in the business, he was at odds with his target market and the subsequent compelling message he wanted to present. I felt proud when I saw Mark's newly created brochure. He used our process expertly in defining himself. His differentiation was evident.

"Leo, I can't even explain to you how my life changed over the course of a few hours. From waking that morning to my normal routine of talking with Joanne, working out and getting dressed for work. To giving her a good-bye kiss, which later proved to be our last good-bye forever. Then dialing 911, desperately giving her CPR, answering questions from the medical examiner, and watching my father-in-law crying while looking at his daughter through the window of the ambulance. Choosing a funeral home, making decisions on an obituary notice, selecting a casket, and visiting the cemetery to purchase cemetery plots for both of us. Who would have thought all of this could have happened in such a short period of time?"

Mark talked about how this life-changing tragedy was affecting everything around him. His thoughts about the changes to his daily life, his future, his perspective on business, his clients and philosophies will continue to shape his future. His beliefs have changed. Yours could, too.

In his book, *Seven Habits of Highly Effective People*, Steven Covey says to begin with the end in mind. Why, as a part of an exercise, are we asked to focus on the end of our lives? Obviously, to give us greater clarity and a sense of purpose to implement the things important to us now, rather than later. How will we want to be remembered? What do we want our spouses, significant others, kids, friends, business associates and community members to say about us? Talk about intro-spection and tough things to work on!

But that clarity keeps you on task. It keeps you focused. It keeps you passionate about living your life today. September 11, 2001 continues to have that kind of impact on us now. Don't wait for tragedy to happen to change your thinking. Go back and re-read Dr. Phil's questions in our Preface and revisit your busi-ness beliefs now.

The Question Unfolds

Remember, as I have been noting, a prospect or client will not always ask you a Value Ladder question verbatim or outright. So you have to be prepared for questions that are worded dif-ferently, but essentially ask, "Why Do You Do What You Do?" Again, they might ask things like:

What has led you to do what you are doing today? Why do you feel this is the best way to help someone achieve his or her goals? Tell me why you feel so strongly about what you do. Give me a compelling reason why you are in this business. What have you learned from this business?

You might reply to the last question like this, "Having been in the business for 15 years, I've seen markets like these. I've learned a lot over the years from working with valued clients like you. I believe you really need a serious focus on the long-term right now. I also believe that diversification of your port-folio is critical, and this is achieved correctly through a good asset allocation model."

What you will find is that you are now "telling a story." It's much like a feature film that's moving along. Your goal is to provoke your prospect into asking further questions such as, "That's interesting. Tell me more about that," or, "What do you mean by that?"

Individual and Organizational Business Beliefs

For me, I do what I do because I truly believe certain truths. I have five core business beliefs. They form the compelling story of my business. They totally support my UVP and, as you will see in the next chapter, link perfectly to my process.

Be specific when you define your business beliefs. For instance, be precise in numbering and ordering them. You should know whether you have four, five, six or however many. Don't take this for granted. Here are mine to serve as examples:

1. I believe that we are still in the midst of a value revolution. This kissing cousin of quality is alive and well. As the noted poet and playwright Oscar Wilde said, "The world is filled with people who know the price of everything and the value of nothing." You probably know some people like this.

2. I believe the changing client is driving the value revolution. They have many characteristics, most notably, more competitive options.

3. I believe our business is becoming more commoditized and the challenge to distinguish ourselves today is critical. There is a client dilemma today due to all the competitive options. With increased acquisitions, mergers, and consolidations, everybody wants to own the client's wallet. To the changing client, everybody looks the same and talks the same. But as acclaimed Harvard Business School professor Theodore Levitt said, "There is no such thing as a commodity. All goods and services are differentiable." (Marketing Imagination, *Harvard Business Review*) I believe the client dilemma is further challenging us to correctly distinguish ourselves based on our value.

We need to be **distinct**, or we will become **extinct**.

4. I believe that any organization or team/individual in business today needs to answer seven simple yet powerful questions to truly distinguish themselves based on their value. We call these questions the Value Ladder because we believe answering them all embodies the full essence of your organizational and/or team/individual value.

5. I believe we must stop winging our responses to clients and answer questions with confidence, passion and speed. To truly distinguish yourself you should develop world-class answers to the most important thing you have to sell...YOU. These answers need to be delivered with the highest levels of confidence, passion and speed (remember, it's not quickness of speech, but lack of hesitation in response).

These are my core business beliefs. You'll notice I didn't say anything about my own passion, commitment, respect, trust or value. That's because those things provide the answers to how I am *individually* different. They reflect core values that I live my life by, and that my company also lives by. These core values are different from my business beliefs.

Some of the most compelling stories to share with people are your business beliefs. Let's say you are a money manager. Nicholas-Applegate's investment philosophy brands them as a growth manager. They have their own compelling story of their investment philosophy. The organization understands the importance of having their own set of core business beliefs. They not only have to sell the business beliefs from a firm-wide perspective, but they also have to look at their marketplace in ways to distinguish themselves to financial consultants around the globe.

They also believe it's important to know what the future has in store, and their four business beliefs reflect their vision. The Nicholas-Applegate team must meet with FEs and deliver their business beliefs in a consistent fashion. They say, in essence, "We believe we are in the midst of a fee-based paradigm, and we believe you must separate yourselves as trusted FEs." It becomes a compelling story, so the unique solutions they present help bring those beliefs alive.

Another good example of business beliefs comes from Steve Gresham, the Chief Sales and Marketing Officer of the Private Client Group, Phoenix Investment Partners, Ltd. Prior to joining Phoenix, Steve was the president of his own company that specialized in the needs of affluent investors and their FEs. At that time Steve asked me to review his answers of distinction for inclusion on his new website.

Here were five of Steve's seven business beliefs:

We believe that: Tactics Replace Strategy as Keys to Success – While we contribute actively to the strategic plans of our wealth management clients, our strength is in the development of better tactics to improve execution. We work best with clients who have a clear vision of their goals and objectives and seek to refine their approach.

We believe we need to: Tune in to All Distribution Channels – Our clients benefit from our experience at all five of the major distribution points in the wealth management industry: brokerage firms, private banks, insurance companies, independent advisory firms, and professional service companies servicing accountants.

We believe we need to: Have a Global Perspective – Nearly 20% of our revenue is derived from assignments beyond US borders. Our experience in Canada dates back to 1980 and we have served clients in Europe, Latin America and Asia Pacific. Our clients are well positioned to benefit from increasing globalization of financial services.

We believe we need to: Strive to be the Best – Our clients expect and receive the most current tactical expertise. The Gresham Company and its principals are recognized industry authorities evidenced by our invitations to address key industry conferences, and through our articles in *On Wall Street, Investment News,* and other financial services publications.

We believe we need to: Be Product Savvy – Our clients' success is ultimately reflected in the sale of products and services to HNW and UHNW investors. In order to fully understand these products and services to maximize the potential of any assignment, we maintain expertise in all forms of managed account and fee-based services.

If you've had the pleasure of hearing Steve speak, or if you have read his new book, *Attract and Retain the Affluent Investor: Winning Tactics for Today's Financial Advisor,* you would hear Steve's compelling message coming through loud and clear. He is an absolute black-belt in our industry. Don't you get that sense from reading his business beliefs?

Ideas are Fuel

Now that I've given you some good examples of business beliefs, you need to start brainstorming about the elements that inform your own answer to "Why You Do What You Do." Here are more examples of what other FEs have listed as their core business beliefs:

- I believe in asset allocation
- I believe people need to be more connected to their dreams
- I believe you can reduce risk through diversification
- I believe that equity builds wealth
- I believe in the investment process
- I believe many people are caught up trying to time the market
- I believe financial success begins with understanding the core values and goals of my clients

Team Up

You may already have a list of ideas, and feel ready to finalize your own set of business beliefs. It might be a good idea to team up with a partner or a colleague so you can both share ideas. Start by presenting your beliefs to this partner the same way you would present them to a prospect. Allow your partner to ask questions (and vice versa) about each of your beliefs. Acting as your prospect gives you a safe environment in which to practice delivering your message.

As your partner asks questions, be prepared to go deeper into each belief concept. This is important. For each business belief and/or key word, ask to be challenged. Be prepared for the follow-up question, "What do you mean by that?" or, "Tell me more," or, "Why do you feel so strongly about that?" Employ the same process here as you did with your UVP.

Once you have identified your business beliefs and have determined they are consistent with where you want to take your business, revisit your UVP and re-write it if necessary. As you did with your UVP, be prepared to do some editing and some critical evaluation of your business beliefs. Now is the time to take out your virtual screwdriver to tighten your thoughts and refine your message.

Your business beliefs must be consistent with the solutions or the process you market. Prospects and clients can spot inconsistencies right away. Some FEs find that their organization's business beliefs are different from their own, e.g., promoting product instead of the investment process. This is time for true reflection about what you believe. It's when you decide how you want to align yourself with the best interests of your clients.

After Who, What, Why – Are You a Fit?

After discussing your background, stating your UVP, and sharing your business beliefs with a prospect, you may discover something very important. You may find there is an incompatibility or a disconnect. Sometimes the chemistry just isn't right. This may not be a relationship either of you want to pursue.

If so, this is ok, because we all need to develop and maintain relationships with those who share our values, beliefs and passions. If a prospect does share your business beliefs, then you can proceed to climb higher on the Value Ladder. By this time the prospect should be eager to hear all about how you do what you do...the next step on the Value Ladder.

Strategic Questions to Consider

Take a few moments to reflect on what you've read in this chapter. Give a lot of thought to what you have written so far about your business beliefs. Before you finalize them, ask yourself these strategic questions to help sum up what you have learned so far:

- What are my core business beliefs?
- Have I prioritized them?
- Where are my business beliefs written or posted?
- Can my team/partner/assistant articulate these business beliefs?
- Can I take my business beliefs to the next level when a prospect asks me, "What do you mean by that?" or, "Tell me more?"
- Can I articulate them with confidence, passion and speed?

- How do my beliefs have an impact on the way I do business?
- Do they help drive my business and keep me in focus?
- Do I use my business beliefs in my marketing and sales materials?
- Do my clients know my business beliefs?
- What impact might they have on my prospect's decision to do business with me?

Remember, it's best to pinpoint exactly how many business beliefs you will ultimately call your own. Be precise. How many of these beliefs can you fit in your virtual file cabinet? You don't want to overload your folder drawer.

As the former balcony preacher (yours truly) challenged his college buddies early on in this chapter, challenge yourself: Do you BELIEVE? Popular recording artist, Chris Isaak said it even better in his song, "I Believe":

> *I believe the stars keep shining all through the night.*
> *I believe if we just keep trying it will be all right.*
> *I believe that someday we're gonna find our way.*
> *And I believe in a beautiful day.*
> *I believe, I believe, I believe. I believe, I believe, I believe."*

Better yet, what do YOU believe?

Now that you have a better understanding of your business beliefs, the next logical question from your clients will be, "How?" or "How Do You Do What You Do?" It's time to climb the Value Ladder to question number four to discover your answer.

$$\left(\text{Keep that screwdriver handy!} \right)$$

mirror mirror on the wall

am **i** the most valued

of them all?

CHAPTER SIX

How Do You Do What You Do?

How Do You Do What You Do?

"It's not what you do.
It's the way that you do it.
That's what gets results."

— Anonymous

Dallas, 1994. I'm in a training session with a small group of FEs, and we're discussing the themes of competing on value, business beliefs, and understanding the Value Ladder process, and all the usual topics. During my presentation, I notice an FE looking at me in a rather odd way. The best way to describe the look on his face is probably like this: It was the old "deer-in-the-headlights" gaze. I thought to myself, "I need to talk to this guy at the break to find out what is going on with him. Either he doesn't like me, or I'm not getting my message across to him."

When I met up with him a while later he confessed, "Leo, I don't know my value. I really don't think I can get the word 'value' out of my mouth. I want to become a better consultant, and I'm committed to fee business. I just need some help."

After more discussion about his goals and other issues, he asked me to visit his hometown to help him work on his over-all approach to competing on value. I left for Tucson a few weeks later where I spent time working with him in some important areas. One of the things we worked very hard on was developing his own process.

The FE's name is Bobby Present, and he wanted to develop a strategy to attract high net worth clients using a proactive CPA referral strategy. He also wanted to align his value as an investment management consultant to the fiduciary needs of Native Americans in the Southwest. During our time together, he learned how to position his value. He increased his confidence level and speed at answering questions, and found his passion.

As a result of the process we developed together, Bobby developed strategic relationships with CPAs that helped him reach his target audience, and he catapulted from being a $200,000 producer to being a $700,000 producer in five years. He now controls $100 million in assets and was featured on the cover of industry trade magazine *Registered Representative.*

Bobby's introspection–as yours will–led him to develop his process of differentiation, appropriately named, *The Present Process.* Bobby developed seven steps. Here they are:

Bobby's Seven Steps

1. Identifying Your Financial Needs and Establishing Goals–The cornerstone of a sound investment strategy begins with the understanding of where the investor is financially, where they want to go and how they can get there. The value of the Present Process is to provide you with a clear understanding of your current and future financial situation, to put your needs into perspective and to define your ongoing financial goals.

2. Developing Your Personal Investment Strategy–Investors seek assistance regarding current asset allocation decisions. They want to understand what to expect in the stock and bond markets. The value of the Present Process is in providing you with an advisor's insight into the Managed Money arena and knowing how to correctly structure a portfolio to meet its designed objectives.

3. Establishing Your Written Game Plan–Investors should develop a customized plan to meet their long-term investment objectives. They expect a recommended plan of action. The value of the Present Process is in designing an Investment

Policy Statement, individually created and uniquely written to meet your individual investment needs.

4. Implementing Your Plan–Investors need assistance in selecting the right investment managers to meet their needs. The value of the Present Process is knowing how to effectively evaluate a Money Manager for consideration and how to correctly select a Money Manager based upon your overall needs and the overall approach of each Money Manager.

5. Maintaining Your Objectives and Reaching Your Goals– Investors need to know if they are on track with their financial goals. They want to be assured that the same plan we've put in place is being correctly followed. Investors demand accountability. The value of the Present Process is providing a structured quarterly review process, complete with re-visitation of goals and analysis of progress to date.

6. Keeping the Promise–Investors want to know that the advisors chosen to manage their funds are doing what they've been hired to do, with the systems they have promised, and with the people they have chosen to manage their portfolio. The value of the Present Process is in becoming a liaison to ensure that no surprises occur and that your funds are managed by organizations practicing what they have promised.

7. Continuing the Commitment–Investors want service second to none. They want to know they are dealing with a committed professional who is providing ongoing expertise to meet their needs. The value of the Present Process is demonstrated by my commitment to this business and, more importantly, to your business. My attitudes, knowledge and skills are constantly focused on the continued growth of your portfolios.

Take a moment to think about these questions:

• What is the value you provide at each step?
• What tools do you utilize to make each step come alive?

- Are there ways you could make each step better?
- What do you call your process?

Learning a Lesson From Bobby

What did you observe from reading Bobby's process? His process includes seven steps—how many do you have? As with your business beliefs, you should list your steps in an orderly fashion. Bobby reiterates his value in a way that reinforces what he does in each step of his process. Have you?

He integrated a few atypical industry words to define his key steps. For example, he uses the term, "Game Plan" instead of investment policy statement in his third step. I love the way Bobby labels his sixth and seventh steps, "Keeping the Promise," and "Continuing the Commitment." You can feel how his heart and soul come through.

As you learned from Bobby's case history, it's all in the process. Do you have a process? Can you explain your process to clients and prospects? If not, how do you expect to develop and grow your business? I'll help you discover and develop a process that will differentiate you from your competition, and help you win more high-level business. We'll go into detail toward the end of the chapter with some important exercises to help you do this.

Now, let's re-visit Nicholas-Applegate and their process from a corporate perspective. They use a four-step "Unique Solutions Process" that evolved from the ways they partner with key FEs committed to growing a fee-based practice.

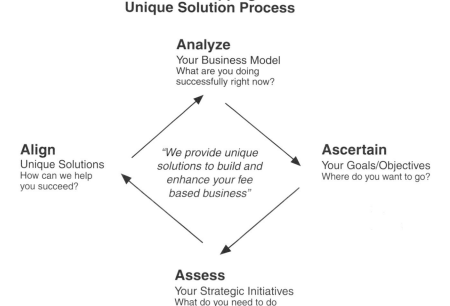

**Nicholas-Applegate
Unique Solution Process**

Analyze
Your Business Model
What are you doing
successfully right now?

Align
Unique Solutions
How can we help
you succeed?

*"We provide unique
solutions to build and
enhance your fee
based business"*

Ascertain
Your Goals/Objectives
Where do you want to go?

Assess
Your Strategic Initiatives
What do you need to do
to get there?

It took a couple of offsite meetings for the Nicholas-Applegate sales team to develop this process. It supports their UVP and business beliefs, and is used selectively with some of their top prospects and clients.

Kissing Cousins of the Question, "How Do You Do What You Do?"

You're in a meeting, you've just explained the first three steps of the Value Ladder, and your prospect says, "Everything sounds great. What's next?" or, "Where do we go from here?" Some prospects may have already talked with two or three of your competitors, and the conversation might go something like this, "I was speaking to a competitor and he said he had a methodology, what's yours?" or, "The FE I spoke to last week had a very comprehensive five-step process. Do you have one?" These are the types of questions that come up when you're on the fourth rung of the Value Ladder. And you will need world-class answers to all of these questions.

Your unique process is a key element of your differentiation. Both you and your prospects have a process: Your prospects use one to make a buying decision; you use one to develop new business relationships and to retain and grow your asset base. When you're making a personal buying decision, i.e., a new house, car, or a family vacation, you have a particular thought process to help you make those decisions.

We all have a pattern to our thinking. Sometimes we are impulsive, but most times we stop and think of the many ramifications before we spend or invest. Prospective clients use the same process. They will ask Value Ladder-type questions, too.

Simply put, **a process is a system of operations or creating something; a series of actions, changes, or functions that achieve an end or result**. Your organization's new business and retention processes can be differentiated from your competition by how well you and/or your team make them come alive. The business idea that "it's not what you do, but how you do it" especially holds true here.

Michael Gerber says it best in his book, *The E Myth Re-Visited*: systems are the key. He discusses taking everything you do and developing a system, or process, around it.

Most successful, committed FEs already have a process. But I've known many high level FEs who do not. They just wing it. I've seen million-dollar producers at my retreats who've said, "I'm here because after hearing your presentation at a seminar, I realize I don't really have a process, or a way to properly deliver it."

Delivering it means illustrating it—not just describing it—and going through the steps of bringing it to life. For example, can you graphically walk a prospect through your process? Go to your flip chart and start drawing. Use your imagination. A picture is worth a thousand words. (How many times have you heard this?) Illustrating your process helps solidify its value through visuals and storytelling.

Your Process—Create It, Make it Come to Life, Spread the Word

Ok, now it's time to define your process. In my training sessions I ask participants to brainstorm all the things they believe are part of their process. To help generate ideas I ask, "What would you say to a prospect if he or she asked, 'What is your process?'"

Start thinking about (or listing) components of your process. These may include steps like:

- Long-term goals discussion
- Disciplined approach
- Discovery
- Evaluation
- Constant monitoring
- Asset allocating
- Performance reporting
- Planning
- Protection

Next, take a look at the chart to the right.

I call it the "Client Relationship Process." Study the four areas for identifying your process.

Column one allows you to list up to 10 steps in your process that differentiate you from your competition (you may only have four or five steps).

Client Relationship Process

1: STEP-BY-STEP	2: HOW DO WE GO ABOUT DOING THIS?	3: DIFFERENTIATION FACTORS	4: ADDING MORE VALUE
Step 1			
Step 2			
Step 3			
Step 4			
Step 5			
Step 6			
Step 7			
Step 8			
Step 9			
Step 10			

Column two asks for your explanation of each step in your process: What are the specific actions you need to take to complete each step? How do you make these actions come alive?

For example, if you are a financial planner, what are the specific things you do for a client with asset allocation? Do you use a firm-recommended approach or do you use third-party software? Do you ask certain types of questions? List all of these things you do.

Column three is where you list all of the ways you or your organization are different from the competition. This step is more difficult to analyze. Think of your core competitors—is there a benchmark that sets you apart? Do you have any idea of their process?

Column four allows you to include additional ways you or your organization can add more value within each step for your prospects and clients. Is there anything in your process that you can change to make it even better? Authors Robert J. Kreigel and Louis Patler challenge readers in their book title, *If It Ain't Broke...Break It!* Sounds like the kind of unconventional wisdom that just might work in a changing world.

So, instead of just saying to your prospect, "Yes, I have a five-step process." I say to you, "Let's go to Process School, and really get down to your differentiation. Let's take each step so deep that, by the end, you'll feel as though you have your doctorate in Process."

You alone make this process come alive; prospects are buying YOU. All of the steps in the process are like your arms, your legs, different parts of your body. You are the most important reason a prospect will make a buying decision. You make this buying decision a memorable experience for them. Then, as a bonus, this prospect becomes an advocate because they feel so good in this relationship.

It's like being a golfer. A golfer might say, "I really have to get good at the short game, I have to get better at hitting my driver or my fairway woods, my irons, my course management." They have to work and practice to become the consummate professional. It works the same way for you. You may have five steps in your process, but the problem—as I see it—is that most FEs just take them all for granted. Because the steps become so automatic, and you're so familiar with them, some of the excitement starts to wear away.

Many times you will hear that your prospect is talking to a competitor with the same process. So what should you say? Most times, it may be *how* you say something rather than *what* you reply. In this situation, here's what I would say to a prospect who said that to me. "Well, Mr. Ideal, I'm glad to hear you're speaking to an FE who espouses a process. Anyone you talk to should be able to look you in the eye and properly explain how they will work with you, and what you should expect."

Say it with passion, in a way that makes your prospect feel good about it. That way, you reinforce that he's right to be doing his homework and that you would expect no less from him. But when you follow up with your own story, make it come alive for him with your delivery of confidence, passion and speed.

Make sure to complete at least the first two columns of the Client Relationship Chart to get your hands around your process. The last two steps (three and four), may take some time to complete, but keep thinking about what makes your process differentiable, and how you can make the steps of your process even more powerful and take them to another level.

Don't Take Anything for Granted

On each of the chart's sections, go as deeply as you can. Don't take for granted that anything you do is implied or obvious. Think about it. Many of the things you do for clients you likely take for granted. Once you write them all down, you'll be surprised at the level of service you actually provide—or don't provide.

Now that you have a formal process, you understand the objectives, and can implement each step, here is another point. The last step of your process should set the stage for your retention strategy and focus on a "service" theme. This step might include these types of actions:

- Sustaining the commitment
- On-going communication
- Coaching to meet lifetime financial goals
- Monitoring the plan or the portfolio
- Evaluating and reporting on the plan or portfolio

This is also a good time for you to consider how to keep and grow your clients for life. What behaviors increase the probability of developing lifetime clients? For example, if a client asks you, "Now that I'm a valued client, what should I expect from you?" they are, in essence, trying to understand your retention and growth process.

- Do you have a retention and growth process?
- How can elements of this process be included in the last step of your existing client relationship process?

Once you've had time to refine your client relationship process, take out your virtual screwdriver and begin tightening. It's a good idea to review your earlier Value Ladder answers. Does your newly developed process give you any ideas that would improve your unique value proposition or your business beliefs? Should you add, delete or emphasize words or phrases in your previous steps?

How can you add more value? Can you go deeper? Place the descriptive information in your manila folders in the virtual file cabinet and you'll find when you refer to it–in situations you may never have dreamed of–you'll be smiling to yourself.

What to Name the Baby

Now that you have your process well thought-out, your steps are in order, and you've come up with some ideas that would add more value, what will you call it? Your process should have a name; otherwise it's just another generic presentation. A name breeds recognition and branding.

Those of you who have children may remember the challenge of trying to come up with a name. Maybe you already knew what you wanted–you and your spouse were in total agreement. Or maybe the baby was in your arms and you were still trying to decide. But once you did, the name seemed absolutely perfect.

When you come to grips with your final decision, you become even more convincing and your message is even more compelling.

Bobby Present's process is simply called, The Present Process."
Nicholas-Applegate's process is called, "The Unique Solutions
Process." Mine is called "The Value Ladder Process."

What are you going to call yours?

The higher you climb the Value Ladder, the closer you get to
establishing a good rapport with your prospects, and the more
they will feel comfortable and committed to you. The more you
share, the more you communicate, the closer you become. It's
a great feeling. Never forget: YOU are the Process. It's **How
You Do What You Do.**

Strategic Questions to Consider

Does your organization have a formal client relationship
process for a new business relationship? If yes:

- What are the objectives of each step?
- How do you implement each step?
- What are the benefits of each step?
- What differentiates you from the competition at each step?
- Have you branded or trademarked your process so it is
  distinctly yours?
- How well can your team communicate the process?
- Why is it important that your prospects understand
  your process?
- What benefits can your organization realize if the team
  clearly communicates the process?
- How can you help your team communicate the process?

You're now ready to climb the Value Ladder to question
number five, "Who Have You Done It For?"

Let's start analyzing your client successes!

mirror mirror on the wall

am **i** the most valued

of them all?

CHAPTER SEVEN

Who Have You Done It For?

Superman,
Wonder Woman
to mention only a
few.

Who Have You Done It For?

If a company understands value
from its customers' perspective,
ways usually are found to deliver that
value to their satisfaction.

— Robert B. Woodruff and Sarah F. Gardial,
Know Your Customer

As I've been repeating to you throughout the book, clients are changing. More than ever, you must listen to what they are telling you in order to analyze their issues, understand their emotions and provide solutions. Here is what they are saying:

- I am more informed
- I have greater choices
- I am more enlightened
- I want to know what I am getting for my money
- I can bypass the traditional only-game-in-town suppliers
- I am less swayed by marketing gimmickry
- I am more selective
- I have competitive options

You and I also are among this group of changing clients. Look in your own mirror again and reflect on the changes in your life. It probably amazes you to think about your life continuum, and the key events that have impacted your personal and professional life.

This chapter will help you be more introspective, looking at your relationships with those key people who help "pay your bills" and allow you to live the life you lead. Those special people are called clients. I want you to really think about these individuals and take the time to evaluate the success you have had with them.

I recently completed a client workshop and a story resonates that's worth mentioning. Scott, a key member of a one-million dollar production team from a regional brokerage group, asked if I would be interested in coaching his team. He was inquisitive about our process. He asked:

- What would you do first, Leo?
- Where would you focus?
- What can I expect from your work?
- What is your process?

Doesn't this sound familiar? Remember reading this in the previous chapter?

We were riding in a golf cart before the company's golf outing and I said, "Scott, tell me about your clients." He responded, "What do you want to know?" So I said, "Who is your ideal client? Who really pumps you up? Who do you really enjoy working with the most? Who really appreciates your value? Who are you proud to say is your client? Who gives you goosebumps when you talk about them to others? Who, if you could multiply this client by 100, would give you the ultimate client base for your practice? Describe this client to me, Scott, and tell me about the success you've had with that client."

It was interesting to see his response. I only wish I had a digital camera to capture his expression because it was one of a pained successful practitioner who literally was dumbfounded. "I don't know," he said. "That's the problem. How do we even figure it out? We're just not sure. It's probably one of the key issues holding us back because we are paralyzed without a creative marketing strategy. Who do we deliver our UVP, business beliefs, and process to? Who should we be telling our compelling story of value to in the future?" he asked.

This encounter hit a nerve with me.

You see, I'm from the school that teaches us to create our own future. I've even developed hypothetical classes and theoretical degrees for myself like my "Introduction to Clients" course, which focused on the questions, "Who do you want to have as your clients?" My MBA in "Advanced Client Relationships" taught me about going narrow and deep with my focus. My thesis on "Client Success" focused on creating a culture of lifetime clients. Key doctoral coursework in my "Personal University" emphasized alignment of my value and my values with my clients', the understanding of lifetime value, and the real meaning of growth and retention of these clients. It also taught the concept of obtaining referrals without ever having to ask for them (contrary to current referral gurus' thinking today), and the constant quest for the answers to the ultimate introspective client questions.

I remember hearing Nasdaq CEO Hardwick ("Wick") Simmons (formerly Prudential Securities president and CEO) eloquently challenging his troops at a major conference with a perfect question of introspection. He said, "Are *you* convinced that your *clients* are convinced that you add value?" Wow! I sat in the back of the room and wanted to applaud his challenge. I knew, though, from experience that the majority of that meeting's attendees could not answer the question.

A Business of Confidentiality

Translating what you do into meaningful terms for your prospects and clients is best achieved by sharing how you have added value to meet your clients' unique needs. Who you do business with is, of course, a private matter between you and your clients. Sharing the specifics of a client's personal situation is not something you want to do. But you can still use former and current client successes in your favor. You can go into your virtual file cabinet and pull out the stories you need, when and where appropriate.

You can also describe your clients to a prospect by focusing on market segments you serve like high net worth individuals, corporate executives, small business owners, physicians, foundations, endowments, or corporate treasurers of 401(k) plans. That way you will not divulge any confidential information and your current client relationships are protected. You will come across as professional, and still fully describe your solutions and the real value you added in each situation.

Tools to Help You Analyze Your Clients and Markets

Here's what the fifth step on the Value Ladder does for you: It forces you to think in deeper layers about your clients, about who they are, and whether your interests are aligned with theirs. It makes you think, "Which new clients would I like to work with?" Do your current clients have an appreciation for your value and your process, and are they willing to pay you for it? This exercise will also force you to think about whether or not you want to continue working with certain clients.

I have two great tools, among others, in my *Discovering Your Value* workbook I'd like to share with you. The first is a chart called the "Individual Client Analysis." Here, you can break your analysis down into four key elements:

1. Who are your individual clients?
2. What are their key emotional issues?
3. What are the solutions for these issues?
4. What is the real value you provide?

The second chart is called the "Market Segment Analysis." One focuses on individual clients, while the other focuses on specific target markets.

This is a great exercise for you. Take some time and write down the names of your top clients in the first column on the *Client* chart, and some of your target markets in the first column of your *Market* chart.

Individual Client Analysis

1: INDIVIDUAL CLIENTS	2: KEY EMOTIONAL ISSUES Challenges – Circumstances Concerns – Frustrations Opportunities – Needs Problems	3: SOLUTIONS	4: REAL VALUE

Market Segment Analysis

1: MARKET SEGMENT	2: KEY EMOTIONAL ISSUES Challenges – Circumstances Concerns – Frustrations Opportunities – Needs Problems	3: SOLUTIONS	4: REAL VALUE

The next column, Key Emotional Issues, (on both charts) is very important to study. Why? Because the best way to learn how to sell is to first understand what it is like to buy. That great sales adage says it all. How well do you really understand your clients' emotions? Your clients and prospects each have various challenges, circumstances, concerns, frustrations, opportunities, needs, and problems. We call these the Seven Key Emotional Issues. This segment forces you to think about how well you know your clients and markets.

What key emotions have you attended to lately?

I also refer to these emotional issues as driving and restraining forces. Driving forces are positive factors that lead you to–or drive you toward attaining business and personal goals. Restraining forces are negative factors that could potentially hold you back from the achievement of your big picture goals. They are like having handcuffs on with no key. You struggle, you squirm, you are emotionally in knots. The more you can *relate* to your client's emotions, the better you can emotionally *connect* with them.

Here is a complete listing of the Seven Key Emotional Issues:

Driving Forces (Positive Factors) and Restraining Forces (Negative Factors)

1. Challenges: Things that inhibit the client from achieving goals. Example: "Market volatility is challenging our ability to meet our long term portfolio needs."

2. Circumstances: A situation that accompanies an event. Example: "My wife's father is seriously ill and in need of personal in-home care."

3. Concerns: Issues of interest or importance. Example: "She may have to quit her job."

4. Frustrations: Issues causing the client to feel disappointed or unfulfilled. Example: "We just never seem to get ahead. There is always something holding us back"

5. Needs: What the client wants or requires. Example: "Our children will be entering college over the next two years. We need funds for tuition, and maybe for Dad's care".

6. Opportunities: Situations favorable to the attainment of a goal. Example: "We just won $20,000 in the Lotto/or we may be inheriting money from an estate."

7. Problems: Questions raised out of concern or doubt. Example: "Will I lose my money in the stock I bought two years ago?"

The best way to understand your clients' emotions is, first, to understand your own.

You might, for example, be in an emotional situation where you realize one of your *challenges* is that you are so busy managing the growth of your practice that you don't have time to leverage and annuitize more.

So, what are some of your emotional issues?

One of my *concerns* might be that I became ill and couldn't effectively do business, or that something happened to one of my partners. And what's a *circumstance* that might be an issue for me? Perhaps it's writing this book among all of the other responsibilities I have and not letting anything slip through the cracks.

A Case Study to Consider

I was coaching my long-time friend Lori Van Dusen, a high-level investment management consultant at Salomon Smith Barney. I met her during my days at Elias Asset Management

112

where I worked with my friend and mentor, David Elias. My first impression of Lori goes back to our initial meeting and still holds true today. Lori is in my personal Hall of Fame. She is as good as it gets in the business: Total class, a consummate professional, dedicated to her profession, a builder and leader of a world-class team, CIMA designated, and competitively intense. She balances all this with her commitment to her two sons, her husband Ron, and her passion for running.

During my consulting assignment with Lori and her team, I asked another friend, Jeff Liebel, president of Counterpoint Consulting in Williamsville, New York, to provide some expert diagnosis and evaluation of her team members. Eventually, Jeff and I were asked to present a Harvard Business School-type case study on Lori's practice to her peers at one of the major annual conferences sponsored by her firm. The attendees are the "best of the best" investment management consultants in the industry. Take a look at the session overview that Jeff and I prepared:

Session Overview

The purpose of this session is to help practice leaders deal with the real issues of strategizing and building their businesses. The interplay of opportunity, potential, personal desire and the players of the team come together to produce an outcome. Is it the outcome you want–or does it need to be something different?

Successful practice builders all seem to follow a similar path in the personal transition they go through in pursuit of growing the business. There are significant points along the way where critical review and reassessment of the strategy, roles and people is necessary. Lori Van Dusen has built a billion dollar team, but things seemed harder, not easier as this went on. So what now...and what next? Through utilization of objective outside expertise, Lori set in motion the next generation of her business, including changes to her role and that of the team. This session will focus on the process tools and resources she utilized and continues to utilize as she reshapes and builds her business for growth and sustainability.

Does this sound like something you can relate to–or would like to relate to–when you reach two billion dollars-plus in assets under management? And how does this story relate to the issue at hand: client successes and the seven emotional issues we've identified?

Lori is a leader who practices what she preaches. She took the time to address the seven emotional issues, answering them in two ways: She used one list for her personal emotional issues, and another for her business emotional issues. Lori is a "Michael Jordan" in this business and I can tell you first-hand how emotionally drained she became from her own honest introspection.

Remember, understanding your own emotions first tends to improve your empathic listening skills. Instead of just "hear-ing" your prospects, you actually "listen" better. You acknowl-edge them with respect, and your connection to that person strengthens dramatically.

Try the exercise for yourself. List your own answers to your personal and business emotions. Then think of some of your top clients to determine how well you've emotionally connect-ed to them. Are you as successful as you thought you were?

You really need to take the time to talk to–and listen to–your clients. Some FEs get so busy throwing products at clients that they don't get to know them or their key emotional issues. And this is a critical aspect of client analysis.

Think About Your Solutions

Once you've had time to discover all of the issues your prospects and clients may be dealing with, it's time to deliver solutions (column three). (Make sure you look at both charts

Examples of **Driving Forces** (Positive Factors) and **Restraining Forces** (Negative Factors) for yourself:

Challenges: _____

Circumstances: _____

Concerns: _____

Frustrations: _____

Needs: _____

Opportunities: _____

Problems: _____

Examples of **Driving Forces** (Positive Factors) and **Restraining Forces** (Negative Factors) for your client:

Challenges: _____

Circumstances: _____

Concerns: _____

Frustrations: _____

Needs: _____

Opportunities: _____

Problems: _____

and analyze both clients and markets.) The solutions could be related to wealth management, tax planning, or financial planning, for instance.

When you start thinking in terms of solutions, then you also begin thinking in more comprehensive, consultative terms instead of selling product. You're also thinking about being a problem-solver to your clients, which would be another value-added component in your differentiation.

And don't forget all that work you've done defining the uniqueness of your solutions in the UVP exercise. Is the work I challenged you to do in Value Ladder question number two connecting here as well? It should be. Are your solutions truly comprehensive? Are they integrated? Personalized? Customized? Get the picture?

The more you work on these concepts, the more they transform from threads of information into a tight rope...a rope that is strong, built on conviction and integrity, and which represents the most important thing you have to sell, the person in the mirror...YOU!

Continuing on, column four of the chart is Real Value. What is your real value? This area helps to ensure that your real value is realized. Here you need to think about your clients, think about their emotions and the issues they are struggling with, and the solutions you are currently providing. When you eventually reach the seventh step on the Value Ladder, you'll have more insight as to the value you provide your clients and prospects, and you'll be better equipped to fill out the Real Value area.

Consider this Scenario

Think about the biggest, most important prospect you are working with right now. Consider the one that could possibly "make" your career. The one who could make an impact on your business, taking it to a higher level. This prospect is one you really covet; one you would be proud to say is a client of yours. Write down the name of this prospect.

Now, if your prospect were to ask you for a reference, which clients would you have that prospect call? Are these clients part of your top 10 list? Are they key clients? What questions do you think your prospect might ask your key clients about you and your company?

Three key questions for your key clients to answer:

Key Clients	Why did you decide to do business with...	What do you value the most about...	What is the real value that... has provided to you

If I were to pick up the phone and call some of your key clients, I would ask them the following key questions:

1. How long have you been working with your FE?
2. What, specifically, is he/she doing for you?
3. Why did you decide to do business with your FE?
4. Tell me what process you went through to make your decision.
5. Who else did you consider?
6. What do you value most about your FE?
7. Do you trust your FE?
8. What is the *real value* that your FE provides?

117

Many times, you will find that your clients will answer that they have emotionally and intellectually connected with you. That's what you want to hear. You can never do too much introspection on your relationship with key clients. Existing clients are the core of your future. Especially your "A" clients. Always remember, it is a lot easier to keep and grow an existing valued client than it is to prospect for another one.

Acres of Diamonds

This is my all-time favorite story to relate the concept of client success. The late Earl Nightingale–the world-renowned success motivation guru–eloquently tells the Acres of Diamonds story on the Nightingale-Conant "Lead the Field" audiotape series. This brilliant true story says it better than anything I've ever heard. Here is a transcript:

"The story is an account of an African farmer who heard tales of other farmers who had made millions by discovering diamond mines. These tales so excited the farmer that he could hardly wait to sell his farm and go prospecting for diamonds himself. So he sold his farm and spent the rest of his life wandering the continent searching unsuccessfully for the gleaming gem that brought such high prices in the markets of the world. Finally, worn out and in a fit of despondency, he threw himself into a river and drowned.

Meanwhile, back at the farm, the man who had bought the farm happened to be crossing the small stream on the property when suddenly there was a bright flash of blue and red light from the stream's bottom. He bent down and picked up a stone. It was a good sized stone, and after admiring it, placed it on his mantel as an interesting curiosity. Several weeks later, a visitor picked up the stone and looked at it closely and nearly fainted. He asked the farmer if he realized what he had found. The farmer said no, he thought it was a piece of crystal. The visitor told him he had found one of the largest diamonds ever discovered. The farmer told the visitor the creek was full of such stones.

Needless to say, the farm the first farmer had sold so that he might find a diamond mine, turned out to be the most productive diamond mine on the entire African continent. The first farmer had owned, free and clear, acres of diamonds, but had sold them for practically nothing in order to look for them elsewhere. The moral is clear: if the first farmer had only taken the time to study and prepare himself to learn what diamonds looked like in their rough state, and since he already owned a piece of the African continent, to thoroughly explore the property he had before looking elsewhere, all of his wildest dreams would have come true."

Complete the following chart. This will help you to gain a greater understanding of how well you know your clients. It will also give you a greater clarity as to the success you are having with each client and where further opportunities may exist.

"ACRES OF DIAMONDS"

Clients	Assets $ you control	%	Revenue $ you are paid	ELV	IPS	CPA	✔	Attorney	✔	Referrals	How would they describe my value?
1.											
2.											
3.											
4.											
5.											
6.											
7											
8.											
9.											
10.											

% = % of total client assets you control
ELV = Estimated Lifetime Value
IPS = Investment Policy Statement

Clients for a Lifetime

What so profoundly struck me about this story was the idea that we are all standing in the middle of our own acres of diamonds.

If we have the wisdom and patience to effectively and intelligently explore the work in which we are now engaged, to explore ourselves, we can usually find the riches we seek.

I've developed my own Acres of Diamonds exercise to help you evaluate your client successes. I suggest you start with your Top 10 clients and then extend it to your Top 25, then Top 50 and ultimately to your Top 100. You can rank your top clients by assets under management, or choose the column to reflect your own personal solutions, i.e., insurance, tax, audit, financial planning, etc. List the percentage of your client's business in the area of expertise.

Next is revenue. I prefer this approach for ranking purposes. Some advisers actually go deeper with profitability analysis. Remember, the deeper you can go, the better for analyzing client successes.

The next column is unbelievably revealing–Estimated Lifetime Value (ELV). "And just what is the estimated lifetime value of your clients?" I might ask. During training sessions, I usually get a lot of the "deer in the headlights" looks at this point. This column represents one of those great "AHA's" as the light bulbs get even brighter.

"What do you mean by estimated lifetime value, Leo?" someone asks. Before I answer, I choose someone from the audience I guess will probably be in the business for a long time and say, "So, Scott, how long will you be in this business? 25 years? Great! Let's assume your client is Mr. Ideal. You are managing $1 million in assets, you have 100% of his assets under management, and you earn $10,000 a year in fees from this relationship. Are you with me so far?

"Okay, Scott, so what will Mr. Ideal be worth to you over the next 25 years?" Gulp. Sweaty palms. "Well," says Scott, "25 years x $10,000–let's see, that will be about $250,000." I say, "No, not exactly, Scott. How else can Mr. Ideal grow with you?

120

Give me five ways. Appreciation? Good, that's one. Capital additions? Good, that's two."

I continue, "Intergenerational wealth transference? Good that's three. Referrals? That's four." Scott says, "That's it, I guess." Then I say, "No, Scott, there's one more. With an improved UVP supported by tight business beliefs, a unique and comprehensive process, you may, in fact, consider raising your fees at some point. Your new message of value should be greatly appreciated by your clients."

"Remember, Scott, if you're not providing any value but are getting paid, that's thievery; if you are providing value but not getting paid, that's philanthropy; if you are providing value and getting paid, well, Scott, that's what it's like to be a financial entrepreneur in this new millennium."

Then I add, "You'll realize that pricing your value can only be accomplished if you know your value. So, Scott, back to Mr. Ideal. What's he really worth? 25 more years in the business, $10,000 plus a year in revenues, add on the five AHA's of estimated lifetime value? What do you have? (Bigger gulp. Sweat all over your body.) Mr. Ideal may be worth close to $2,500,000-plus to your career over the next 25 years."

So, to conclude, I say to him, "Scott, do you have an investment policy statement for yourself? Or your own comprehensive financial plan? You know, the one you sell to others? Do you practice what you preach?" If Mr. Ideal has one, put a checkmark on the chart. List his CPA and his attorney and put a checkmark next to their names if you have met these centers of influence face-to-face and have explained the value you are providing to your mutual client."

You might want to add a "retention" factor to your chart, too. Rate Mr. Ideal in terms of retaining his long term business. A 1.0 rating means you are 100% certain that his assets are staying with you. He is "in the safe."

Give this exercise an honest appraisal. Do it by yourself, then bring your team together. You'll be amazed at your answers, and I guarantee that your honest dialogue with this and the next Value Ladder steps will be some of the most important time you will ever invest in your business.

Strategic Questions To Consider

- Who are my clients?
- How many do I have?
- Are their priorities changing?
- Who should be my clients?
- Do I have a specialization strategy?
- Does it make sense for my marketplace?
- How am I currently adding value to my clients?
- How would they measure my success?
- How can I become their one and only:
  - Financial consultant
  - Investment management consultant
  - Trusted FE
- Are there good ways for me to educate prospects on current client successes?

The strategic implications of answering these questions allow you to focus on the client. You will consider who they are, who they should be, what are their priorities and how they are changing. It will force you to think about your specialization and whether it is well-suited to your current client base. Your introspection will also help you focus on how your clients will measure your success.

With all of this in mind, it is important to understand who your coveted clients are, and more importantly, to understand the successes you have had with them. Only then can you begin to share the answers to, "Who Have You Done it For?" with confi-dence, passion and speed.

Remember, re-visit your virtual file cabinet. You should be ready to reach for drawer #5 with folders labeled, "Your Potential Clients," and "Existing Clients," which will hold appropriate stories that outline your client successes with them. Can you see your file cabinet expanding?

Now, let's move on to the next question, "What Makes You Different?"

$$\left(\text{Time to learn about your umbrella of distinction.} \right)$$

mirror mirror on the wall

am **i** the most valued

of them all?

CHAPTER EIGHT

What Makes You Different?

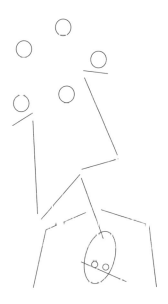

What Makes You Different?

*"There is no such thing as a commodity.
All goods and services
are differentiable."*

– Theodore Levitt
"The Marketing Imagination,"
Harvard Business Review

"So, Leo, what makes *you* different?" I was asked this question during a lunch presentation to a group of FEs. The young FE who questioned me–or better yet, challenged me–in front of his peers waited for a response. I believed it was a challenge because he was pointing his finger at me, and his tone was slightly confrontational. He just wanted me to assure him that I was on top of my own game–and he had every right to ask because he was considering investing his time and money to attend one of my other programs. I couldn't wait to answer.

Have you ever been in this position? You are prepared, on top of your game, and can't wait for the person to finish asking his or her question. You're trying to be respectful, but you're smiling inside. A "smile in your stomach" is what I like to call it. It's like you have a big fishing pole and your bait hits its target. The line moves. "I've got a catch! Let's bring this fish home to papa!" That's how I felt: Respectful, appreciative of the question, and most important, prepared. My confidence, passion and speed were ready to be unleashed.

"Thank you for asking me the question," I said to the FE. (Smiles within.) "I can distinguish myself in three ways. One, through my company versus other competitive alternatives.

Two, with solutions versus other competitive solutions. Three, and most importantly, through my personal level of differentiation. It's what I stand for. It's my set of core values. It's what you can expect from working with me."

I continued, "Where would you like me to focus? My company, my solutions, or what I stand for? Better yet, another way to answer that question—I specialize in helping other committed FEs like yourself answer the very same question: What makes me different? I help you to increase your confidence, passion and speed. Where would you like me to focus?" I asked.

"Uh...uh...uh..., thanks, that's good enough, Leo," he said.

The fish had landed! Please understand that the tone of this dialogue was one of conversational respect—no arrogance, no cavalier approach, nothing condescending. That attitude is not allowed in our programs. We teach consultative, side-by-side selling. True partnering at its best. That's what is needed to properly answer this question.

Perhaps you've encountered a similar situation. Have you ever been directly challenged? When I get to this step in my workshops, I ask the participants if anyone has ever been asked, "What Makes You Different?" I usually get a few chuckles, and some laughter. So, I just continue on and ask the group, "Well, tell me, what other ways can this question be asked?" I usually receive these kinds of answers: "My prospect will say he's talking to another firm, and how does my firm compare?" or, "This other group my prospect is talking to mentioned that they have a program where they work with independent money managers. Do I have a program like that?" or, "What can I expect from working with you as an individual—what are your standards, what will you bring to the table?"

How do *you* feel when you explain how your organization differs from the competition, and how you differentiate your solutions and yourself?

127

You will find that variations of this question tend to arise during competitive dialogue. What's interesting to me about this question is that, many times, senior management believes their reps can answer with authority. "They understand our competition. Don't spend a lot of time on the subject," they say. But it's not until you begin asking competitive questions you can feel the discomfort in their answers. Back to the school of winging it.

Biggest, Baddest and Best Competitor

The answer clients are seeking when they ask the sixth question on the Value Ladder, "What Makes You Different?" is what I call your differentiation. As you read on, you'll learn it involves three specific areas: Your company, your solutions, and you and/or your team.

Most FEs I coach say they need help in this area of knowing their competition. They want information so they can be more knowledgeable, and they also want to know how to articulate issues of differentiation. If you are truly acting and living in an entrepreneurial fashion, you'll realize that the biggest, baddest and best competitor you'll ever encounter is the one looking back at you in the mirror. That's right...YOU. You are your most fierce competitor. After honest introspection, if you can distinguish yourself at a world-class level, well, that's half the battle.

However, I believe you should be conversationally proficient regarding your core–or direct–competitors and their solutions. Again, remember the adage: The best way to learn how to sell is to first understand what it's like to buy. Put yourself in the consumer's shoes. You are now the consumer, or better yet, the changing client. How would you feel in these scenarios?

• You are shopping for a new BMW and stop by a Mercedes dealer. You ask questions about the differences in the two cars. You get vague answers to your questions because the salesman knows very little about the BMW you are in love with.

How do you feel about that?

• You are evaluating custom homebuilders and one of them just can't agree with your dream architectural plans. The other one understands your vision, sits down with you and together you create a plan that is architecturally sound, within budget and ultimately becomes the home of your dreams. How does this make you feel?

• You are checking out two local establishments to determine which one will host your client appreciation seminar. One location understands what you mean by Disney, Nordstrom's, Ritz-Carlton-type service...and they can demonstrate it to you. The other establishment says simply, "Don't worry, we will help you pull it off." How do you feel about that?

How do you think your clients feel when they ask simple questions under the guise of, "What makes you different?" and your response lacks the details they are really interested in hearing? Some FEs say their prospects don't ask this question. But they know prospects are thinking about it, wondering about it, even if they are not asking outright.

This question can be subliminal or couched among other questions during the interview. If you're answering with confidence, passion and speed, they think, "This person has his act together." If, on the other hand, you're winging it then the prospect thinks you don't know your business. You know what I mean. You've been there yourself, as a consumer of other professional services.

The first thing you need to do when your prospect asks, "What makes you different?" is to qualify that question. Ask, "Different from who, different than what?" Tell them you need to better understand what they mean so you can give them the answer they are seeking. Do they mean different from another organization, different in terms of solutions, or different from you as an individual? Do they want to know what they can expect from you through a partnership?

You also can assure them that **the most important decision they will make is whether or not they are comfortable with you and your team.**

By asking your prospect to clarify, "Different from what?" or by using a phrase respectfully like, "Help me to help you," you will be able to focus your answers on the specific differentiation factors the prospect is thinking of. Your response to the prospect's questions will let him or her know the breadth and depth of your differentiation knowledge and will set you apart as world-class.

Remember to always be in the moment. If you've been talking about a certain competitor, and your client asks, "What makes you different?" most likely your response will focus on that competitor. Use your good judgment and intuition. If you feel you are answering a question and you begin rambling, your intuition will tell you that you need to further clarify and confirm the question.

FEs will ask me, "Isn't my UVP a good enough statement of what makes me different?" Well, no. Your UVP is your *proposal of value* to someone. You develop it to the degree that it does, in fact, distinguish you, but at some point more questions will come up about your work. Prospects will want to get deeper into what you will be proposing to them.

It's inevitable that the deeper you go into the dialogue, and the higher you climb the Value Ladder, the more you will have to distinguish yourself. This is especially true as your prospect gets closer to making a decision to invest considerable money, and to partner with you for the long-term. The more a prospect critically analyzes you, the more proficient you need to be at distinguishing yourself at the higher levels.

Sometimes your prospect might jump from, "How Do You Do What You Do?" right into "What Makes You Different?" This happens because many times your *process* will become your *solution.* You'll see how the questions on the Value Ladder tend to build on each other, complement each other, and take answers deeper. This creates a perfect opportunity to go into your virtual file cabinet and pull out the appropriate answers.

Your file drawers should contain manila folders with information on your core competitors, so you also can quickly distinguish yourself at an organizational level. Within those competitor folders you might have additional information on their solutions. You may also have manila folders containing each of your core values, those ultimate levels of distinction that focus on what you truly stand for.

Three Ways to Distinguish Yourself
(Or, Bring Your Umbrella to the Party)

After I broke down the elements of the question, "What Makes You Different" early on in the development of the Value Ladder, I realized there were three key ways to distinguish yourself. Similar to the way I answered this question for the young FE, keep these three points in mind:

You must distinguish your company against competition.
This is called Organizational Differentiation

You must distinguish your company on a solutions level.
This is called Solution Differentiation

You must distinguish yourself on an individual/team level.
This is called Individual/Team Differentiation

During one of my training sessions, I presented these three levels in a great visualization as an umbrella.

When you press the button on a folding umbrella, it pops open,

What Makes You Different?
Differentiate yourself in three ways:

COMPANY

SOLUTIONS

YOU

right? The top of the open umbrella represents your company. All of the metal "spokes" holding up the umbrella represent of the solutions you provide. At this spokes level, you should be looking at your integrated solutions: the products, services, programs or *solutions* you provide to your prospects and clients.

For example, a top consultant in our industry successfully closed on a half-billion dollar family office opportunity. He found success after presenting a solutions package developed from the products and services offered by the newly integrated firm his company became through acquisitions. He offered total integrated solutions. He offered all of the spokes under the company umbrella, and thereby providing unique value to his client. By using his global resources, he offered seamless service in a cohesive manner.

The last umbrella part, but certainly not the least, is the person/team holding up the umbrella. It's the most important person for you to distinguish, the man or lady of the hour...YOU. What do you stand for? What can a client expect from working with you? What are your standards? What is your code of ethics? What are your values?

We will spend appropriate time here developing answers to these questions, as I truly believe **this is the greatest way to distinguish yourself.** The question is: How well can you distinguish *your* umbrella? We'll explore that now by looking at all of the elements: your company, your solutions, and you.

Who Are Your Real Competitors?

I was conducting a session for a major wirehouse and was asked in advance not to spend too much time talking about the competition. "The most important thing is for our FEs to understand that they need to sell themselves," the branch manager said. "I want you to teach them how to do this, so don't worry about spending much time talking about what makes us different from our competitors."

It didn't crystallize for them until we did a follow-up program, that understanding the competition, in fact, is very important when it comes to differentiating yourself. I began asking the FEs at the next session such questions as, "What makes you different from the FE at XYZ Financial Services, Inc?" The managers saw their FEs fumbling for answers.

The FEs needed the verbiage to answer this question with confidence. Nine out of ten times when I ask this question, FEs will say that talking about the competition is a good dialogue to have with their own branch and sales managers because they need the competitive knowledge when talking to prospects. Unless they attend a session like this, however, management and FEs will seldom discuss the issue. Sometimes management feels it has provided enough competitive information to FEs, but more often than not, there is a disconnect between management and FEs.

Before you can answer all of the questions about what makes you different from other firms, you of course need to know who they are and a little bit about them. One of the best ways I've seen for determining who are your key competitors is found in Adrian J. Slywotzky's book, *Value Migration*. He took the concept of a radar screen to help you zero in on your major competition.

The Competitive Landscape

Who are my real competitors?

If a security analyst were following your entrepreneurial organization,
Who would they tell you would be your competitors?
How would they describe the competitive threats?

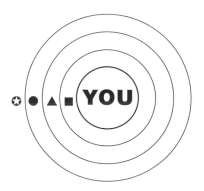

Types of competition:

Direct: ■

Indirect: ▲

Remote: ●

Maybe/Someday: ✪

Slywotzky felt that because business is changing so rapidly, we can't take a myopic approach anymore. He asks these questions in his book:

- Who are your direct competitors?
- Who are your indirect competitors?
- Who are your remote competitors?
- Which ones will be the most important in your industry five years from now?
- Which minor competitors could become immediate threats?

He uses NBC's story as a good example of his radar screen. In his book he asks, "Who would have been NBC's direct competitors 20 years ago?" Well, you might answer ABC and CBS. But if you take it further and think about who their indirect competitors would have been, you might say the telephone, the radio. And who would have been a remote competitor? Maybe a movie theater. Then you consider who might be their competitors today? CNN, Fox, Disney Channel, Pay-Per-View stations, C-span, the Internet, and video stores to name a few.

This example gives you a good idea as to how far your competition actually reaches, and how much it can change over time. If you work with endowments and foundations, for instance, your competition might be small- to mid-sized national consulting firms. If you know of other professionals managing money or providing other services to your clients, then guess what? They are also competitors and should be plotted on your own radar screen.

And just how much information do you need to know about your competition? *Enough to be conversationally proficient.* In other words, you need to be able to look at your prospect eyeball-to-eyeball when they ask you any questions about any of your core competitors and answer at such a level of expertise that your prospects will say to themselves, "This person really has his act together. This person really knows the business. This person understands competitive options... I am dealing with a professional."

It's very important to speak respectfully about your core competitors. Never utter a negative word. You can talk about them in such a way to educate an interested prospect and tell them more than anyone else has, bringing their level of competency even higher about the competitive alternatives just by sharing your knowledge.

You need to be prepared and do enough analysis to be knowledgeable, of course, but not so much that you paralyze yourself. Remember, the most important thing is to be an expert in discussing your own company, your solutions and yourself first. Let's get started breaking down your own umbrella now.

Organizational Differentiation

To begin, give yourself this simple quiz:

- How is Merrill Lynch different from Salomon Smith Barney?
- How is UBS PaineWebber different from Morgan Stanley Dean Witter?
- How is Prudential Securities different from AG Edwards?
- How is Goldman Sachs different from Robertson Stephens?
- How is PricewaterhouseCoopers different from Ernst and Young?
- How is AXA Advisors different from Signator Financial Network?
- How is Capital Guardian Trust Company different from Invesco?
- How is Nicholas-Applegate different from Rittenhouse?
- How is Phoenix Investment Partners different from Roxbury?
- How is Fidelity different from Schwab?
- How is Citicorp different from JPMorgan Chase?
- How is MFS different from AIM?
- How is CIBC different from Nesbitt Burns?
- How is your independent financial planning firm different from a local bank trust department?
- How is MyCFO.com different from a family office in your city?

- How is your wealth management firm different from a private money management firm in your community?
- How is your law firm different from another legal entity in your town?

Of course, for you, the most important question is how your company differs from whomever your prospect is asking about at the moment.

Always remember, if your prospect is investing with someone else by using other financial planning services, or other accounting or legal services–these firms are competitors. Whether they are direct, indirect, remote competitors, or just beginning to fly onto your radar screen, they can encroach upon your business.

Key Competitive Differentiation Concepts

One great way to assess organizational differentiation (which also applies to solution differentiation) is to consider the following concepts as you position your strategy:

The Concept of Uniqueness–As defined in Chapter 4, developing your UVP, uniqueness means exclusive, matchless, or one-of-a-kind. What characteristics make your firm truly unique? Let me tell you about a unique experience I had in this industry that should help you to think about the concept of uniqueness in a few different ways.

I have been on the faculty of my friend Jim Vogelzang's boot camp. Jim was a pioneer in the third party marketing of money managers. Typically, his clients are money managers who need expert sales and marketing representation–Jim's long-term area of expertise. Most of the top institutional money managers sent their key relationship managers to Jim and his unique boot camp.

Have you ever visited a women's prison to spend time on your listening and empathy skills? This was one of the unique experiences Jim provided his participants. Talk about getting perspective on your life. Or how about passing out carnations to strangers during the noon hour in Denver, to simulate the feeling of rejection? Jim's boot camp was unique like that.

Working with his attendees was interesting because many felt their firms were, in fact, not unique. We all seem the same, we look the same, we sound the same, and we smell the same, some asserted. But discovering your uniqueness is a high-five experience. You may have to search long and hard, but the final results may set you in a direction you might never have considered. You are unique, it is only a question of understanding your uniqueness and speaking concisely about it.

The Concept of Competitive Advantages–Most FEs I coach can relate to this. You may not know for certain, but after long deliberations and analysis of your company and solutions, you can usually come up with some powerful points to consider here. It really gets you thinking: Are you truly better than your competition in ways important to your prospect? If you can look in your mirror after studying your competitors and say, yes, you are better, then it becomes strategic. It becomes a competitive advantage that may need to be emphasized in the course of your presentation to prospects. If it's an important issue to your prospect, and you do it better than your competitors, then it becomes a strategic competitive advantage, something on which I put even more emphasis.

The Concept of Parity–In an increasingly commoditized world, we can try our best to distinguish ourselves, but sometimes things seem so similar that they look and feel to be a competitive "wash." Remember here the quotation at the top of the chapter, from Theodore Levitt's "The Marketing Imagination," published in the *Harvard Business Review*: *"There is no such thing as a commodity. All goods and services are differentiable."*

We have a lot of fun in our programs proving this point. I bring a bag of roasted, salted peanuts to a session and pass out a peanut to each participant. "Don't eat it," is my first command. "Let's have some fun." And we always do. "Do you all agree that our business is looking more and more commoditized?" They all agree. "Why the roasted, salted peanut in a shell?" I ask. "Because they, like you, look the same. If they could talk, they would talk the same, walk the same, and smell the same, etc. Well, let's prove the point wrong." I then instruct the attendees to write down as many characteristics as they can about the peanut in their hand. Ready? Set? Go! Watching sophisticated, competitively informed FEs doing this is a hoot.

So, I start pointing to participants: "What did you write down? Yell it out!" I say. "Mine is salty," says one. "Mine has two peanuts in the shell," says another. "Mine has a crack in it," says

The Client's Dilemma
YOU

yet another. The attendees have fun getting outside of their box. I then say, "Now that you've heard what your peers have said, find one more characteristic. Go deeper and have fun." More crazy answers follow. If the group is small, I have even more fun by collecting all of the peanuts. I throw them on a table and say, "Ok, come and claim your peanut now." Lots of laughter and good-natured kidding takes place. This was a great exercise that a former associate taught me; it really works.

And, yes, a competitive person gets upset when they can't find their peanut! What we learn from this exercise is that we *are* different, we *are* unique. Even though we may look the same, when you really study it, we can distinguish ourselves. Another observation I received from an attendee that seemed to sum it up: "You need to pay attention to details. Differentiation is in the eye of the beholder." Can you imagine the dilemma your clients must have?

The Concept of Competitors Uniqueness–This is something that your competitors have an exclusive on. Let's be honest. This is even tougher to compete against, especially if it's one of the key criteria by which your client evaluates you. That said, I'd rather be playing cards knowing what's in my opponents 'hands, wouldn't you? I can then strategize differently and make the most effective use of my resources. You can, too.

The Concept of Competitive Disadvantages–The opposite of competitive advantages, this concept represents what your competitors do better than you. Honest introspection helps here, because it forces you to go deeper into the analysis of your own uniqueness and competitive advantages. Though difficult at times, the process makes you ultimately better and more confident.

Organization Differentiation

Take a look at the table to the right:
- In column one, identify your top five competitors
- In column two, identify your organization's uniqueness
- In column three, identify your own competitive advantages
- In column four, identify the characteristics of your firm and your competitor's firm that you feel are fairly equal
- In column five, identify your competitor's uniqueness
- In column six, identify your competitor's competitive advantages

1: Key Competitors	2: Your Organization's Uniqueness	3: Your Competitive Advantages	4: Parity	5: Your Competitor's Uniqueness	6: Your Competitor's Competitive Advantages
1.					
2.					
3.					
4.					
5.					

Fill in as much as you can. You'll begin to get the language down, and the strategic words will come. You'll start sounding like Tiger Woods. Give it a try.

You may come away with a powerful statement like: "One of the things we are proud of is that our firm has a unique approach to financial planning," or, "We've done a lot of analysis regarding our expertise and solutions, and we truly believe we present many competitive advantages."

Not bad, huh? Sounds pretty good in actual dialogue. Especially after you've done the hard work of analyzing your story.

Solution Differentiation

This concept raises some eyebrows. "You mean I should know more about my competitor's solutions?" Many times participants say, "I don't know what they offer. How would I even find out?" Well, wouldn't you like to have some working knowledge of what you are competing against? I know I do, and it helps me in my positioning.

141

Key Competitor #1 _____

1: Solutions that directly compete against	2: Your Organization's Uniqueness	3: Your Competitive Advantages	4: Parity	5: Your Competitor's Uniqueness	6: Your Competitor's Competitive Advantages

Take a look again at the spokes holding up the umbrella–your solutions. Maybe some of your solutions are liquidity, asset allocation, investment policy statement, trusts, structured products, investment management, or private equity. If you are a fee-based planner, your solution might be your approach to taxes, structuring a customized plan, life planning, or providing values-based solutions. See the chart above.

If I speak to a product expert at a firm, I expect them to educate me not only on their product concentration, but also on key competitors. You have the resources at your firm to get answers. Challenge your management to help you. This should be a key part of their UVP. Call for help. That's what the 800 numbers and direct line access to your internal experts are for.

Last, But Not Least – What Do You Stand For?

Actor Tom Cruise played a sports agent in the hit movie, "Jerry McGuire." During the movie we saw Jerry transform himself from a sleazy, do-whatever-it-takes-to-get-the-business type of guy, to someone with a mission and a developed set of values. One interesting scene in the movie showed the wife of the Arizona Cardinals wide receiver played by Cuba Gooding Jr., going ballistic on Jerry. She bellowed, "What do you stand for, Jerry? What do you stand for?" The important and critical question for you to answer (the most important on your umbrella level of distinction) is just this: What do *you* stand for? What are *your* values?

Can you think of an organization that lives its values? What organization or company or team do you think of? You know what traits I'm talking about: measurable experiences, impeccable service, world-class in everything they do. When participants share their responses with me, you can hear the passion in their voices as they relate their experiences. Companies mentioned earlier continue to pop up: Disney, Nordstrom's, Ritz-Carlton, Lexus and Infiniti.

I love this part of our program because FEs are ready to jump out of their chairs, and sometimes they almost sound like they work for the particular organization they speak of. They are apostles. Passionate advocates. Significant referrers. "Tell me about your experiences with these companies," I ask. "What do they stand for? What value do these companies provide to the marketplace? If I called your top clients, could they list you or your team or your company as one of these organizations? Would they be raving fans? Do they have you in their personal "hall of fame?"

Isn't that your goal? I know it's mine.

Practice What You Preach

I remember visiting an FE's office in Nashville a while back. Behind his desk and over his credenza was a framed list of values with the title, "What I Stand For." I couldn't take my eyes off of it. You could sense this FE's feeling of pride. I knew he *lived* his values.

What I've seen over the years is that many companies will develop broad-based core values for their company. They are called mission statements, value statements, or their beliefs or principles. I'll ask the company, "What are your core values?" And they will say, "We believe in taking care of the client first," or "We believe in customizing solutions for clients." Sometimes when I hear these things, or see them posted in the office, I feel these words are meaningless. Is this just something that the company hired a consultant to put together, or is the company really LIVING it? If they are just words on the wall with no action, then forgive me, they might as well be toilet paper.

Another fun and rewarding moment during our retreats is when we ask participants, after spending two days with each other, to use key words to describe their fellow participants. It's amazing the perceptions we formulate about each other in such a short period of time. Think about the opinions you formulate about the people and organizations you are considering doing business with. Now imagine the perceptions your prospects develop about you in a short period of time.

This is what I call the "Individual/Team Differentiation." If you were asked by your prospect to individually distinguish yourself from a competitor, what would you say? Would you say what you stand for? What are your core values? Your code of ethics? If you bring up your ethics or values, use descriptive words that are passionate.

Always remember, business is first a meeting of the hearts, then it becomes a meeting of the minds. If the most important thing you have to distinguish is YOU, and the most important way to distinguish yourself is by speaking from the heart and connecting with someone else through sharing your standards, code of ethics and core values, it is imperative you have this stuff down pat.

If you really haven't thought too much about your core values in depth, you might want to begin by analyzing them. Are your values internally or externally focused? Are they company values or individual values? Or are they possibly one and the same? Here are some words that may apply to your values, or at least, get you thinking about them:

Sample Values

Abide	Fun	Patience
Ability	Genuine	Perceptive
Accountable	Gracious	Pragmatic
Affable	Heartfelt	Professional
Balanced	Honesty	Rationale
Bravery	Honorable	Reasonable
Caring	Innovative	Reliable
Commitment	Insightful	Respect
Conscientious	Integrity	Safety
Conversational	Intelligent	Serious
Dedicated	Judicious	Sincere
Dependable	Kind	Thoughtful
Education	Love	Trust
Enthusiasm	Loyalty	Value
Expert	Open	Warm
Fairness	Organized	Well-rounded
Forthright	Partner	Wholehearted
Friendliness	Passion	Wise

The most important element of differentiation is literally the *person* the prospect partners with. Even though you can distinguish your company and your solutions, the critical component is YOU. You are the company. You are the process. You are the value.

What Do You Stand For?

I've included a page from my own brochure to give you an example of what makes my company and me different. What are our values? What do I stand for?

Passion: We have boundless enthusiasm and love for our work. For us, work is fun.

Commitment: We have emotional and intellectual commitment to organizational and personal growth. We bring a mind-set of innovative learning and dedication to all of our client relationships.

Trust: We earn this coveted distinction due to our clients' total confidence in our abilities, our integrity and our character. Our clients are confident in us because of our faith in our work and in ourselves. We always do what is right for our clients.

Respect: We treat our clients, and each other, with utmost respect. We regard each client relationship as a special privilege. We are constantly considerate, appreciative and always strive to exceed our clients' expectations.

Value: We are unique because we know our value and constantly strive to understand our client's value. We also believe that value is not only the operative word in business today, but it also is the single, most compelling word that must be in FEs' vocabularies. We are experts at helping organizations compete effectively using the philosophies of value.

So, what do *you* stand for?

A Final Thought About Your Umbrella

Besides being proud that I'm from beautiful Buffalo, and am a masochistic Buffalo Bills fan, I also love the game of golf. Due to our challenging climate, I have a golf umbrella on my golf bag. An umbrella, of course, is used to protect you and your clothing from the rain. Your umbrella of distinction is used in the same way. Use it when you need it.

When the conditions warrant, you take it off your bag and open it. You will feel better protected. Your umbrella of distinction

146

sits in the sixth drawer of your virtual file cabinet. Open your Organizational Differentiation manila folder. Maybe you have files on your key competitors. I do. Maybe you have a manila folder on your solutions or your competitor's solutions. I do. Maybe you have files on what you stand for. I do.

Open your umbrella or your virtual file cabinet when you need it. If you're like me, you'll feel better just knowing it's there, in the event your day or your meeting turns suddenly rainy.

Strategic Questions to Consider

- Who are your real competitors? Which ones do you typically run up against?
- Who do you need to be world-class conversant about? (Minimally, you need to be conversationally proficient.)
- When you think of your typical solutions, is value perceived and realized?
- Do you get excited when you think about the solutions you provide your clients?
- Can your team properly differentiate your business and your solutions from key competitors?
- Does your company have specific values they abide by?
- Do you have individual values you abide by?
- Are your values aimed at your:
    Internal clients?
    - External clients?
    - Both?

Do I hear a drum roll here? We're ready to climb the last step of the Value Ladder, "Why Should I Do Business With You?"

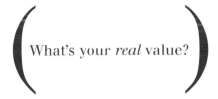

What's your *real* value?

mirror mirror on the wall
am **i** the most <u>valued</u>
of them all?

CHAPTER NINE

Why Should I Do Business With You?

Why Should I Do Business With You?

Try not to become a man of success,
but, rather, a man of value.

– Albert Einstein

We've climbed a long way up the Value Ladder. Can you recall climbing something else and reaching the top? Do you remember that feeling of exhilaration, knowing you really had achieved your goal?

A few years ago, I climbed to the top of Stone Mountain, just outside of Atlanta. I was with my friend and strategic partner, Steve Saenz, president of Paragon Resources. Steve and I went on a business retreat to discuss some opportunities and the possible formation of a new firm. One of the highlights was our strategic walk up Stone Mountain.

I still smile today when I think of how I challenged myself to climb the last hundred yards with thoughts of 'why am I doing this?' in my head. (Not to mention heavy sweat, loss of breath, and utilization of all my best affirmations.) I was Eddie Murphy at his best in the movie, "Nutty Professor," Professor Klump's rendition of "Yes I can," reverberating as my inner chant. About that time, a Jack LaLanne wanna-be ran by us carrying his bike, literally sprinting to the top of the mountain. Steve and I had a good laugh, and my thoughts shifted to, "Oh God, why am I doing this? What's the real value here?"

Obviously, we experienced a lot of real value in that strategic walk. I was with a good friend and partner. We were having a great time, exercising and talking, both about business and about life. We were plotting future opportunities for increasing revenue upside for both our firms. You see, on my walk with Steve, we talked about qualitative issues of importance to us. Things like our life, balance, and control of our future. There were also quantitative issues like new business opportunities, future client growth, and enhanced revenues for our firms.

What is Real Value?

Understanding the concept of real value is a great way to end the climb up the Value Ladder. Just like my climb up the mountain with Steve, you should be at the top of your own Value Ladder mountain now. This thought-provoking mindset should get you thinking about the last question, "Why Should I Do Business With You?" and what is the real value you provide to clients.

Now let's review some other concepts to help us understand the differences in the key themes represented in this book. How is *value*, as used in our UVP, different from *values* as discussed in our previous chapter on differentiation?

Value–The key word in the middle of your UVP is defined as how well your solutions allow you to achieve your client's goals. Remember, it's the proposition of what you do uniquely well. In essence, it tells someone, "Here's what I could do for you." It implies a professional attitude, and that, yes, you are unique. "I am unique, and I do provide value and, get ready– here I come!" It's delivered with confidence, passion and speed.

Values–This is very different from value. Values are qualitative, emotional connectors. They are your standards, your code of ethics. They are what people should expect from working with you.

We end the climb up the Value Ladder with the important concept of *real value* and how it differs from value.

151

Value vs Real Value

Why do we put the word "real" in front of the word "value?" Because it makes it come alive, that's why. The word "real" implies deep meaning. It is complete totality. It is something you need to emphasize. It also is the epitome of what you are presenting to meet your client's needs.

If someone asks me what my value is, I say I help financial entrepreneurs go through a process to discover and articulate their real value. But what is the *real value* of my work? It is the application of my expertise, my specialization, and my core competencies for my clients. **It is the achievement of results, both qualitative and quantitative, they can accrue by working with me.**

Here's a simple, generic example: Take a look at a felt-tip marker. Take off the cap. The cap is a feature. The benefit is that it helps keep the marker from drying out. What's the real value, though? Well, if the marker doesn't dry up, then it lasts longer and you won't have to buy another one so quickly. It will keep your costs down and save you money. Immediately, the benefit extends into something significant to you. The deeper you can extend the benefit, the greater the value, which then becomes real value.

There is a subtle difference between the words value and real value, but the difference is extremely significant. Again, the real value is the *actual application* to the real world. It's not your *claim* of value or something implied. It's explicit. You can prove it. You've done it for others. Prospects can talk to your existing clients and they will verify and validate this value to the fullest. You know you've provided real value when you have tangible success stories of how you've helped others meet their goals.

I always like to ask my prospective clients, "How will you measure my success?" Then I zip my lips and wait for their response. It really tells me a lot about their thought process. I want to know the answer so I can assess how they judge me. How can I exceed the prospect's expectations if I don't know what they are?

• What is the real value they are seeking?
• What is it about my UVP that caught their attention?
• How can I make my value come alive to them so they become one of my passionate advocates?

I am more informed.
I have greater choices.
I am more enlightened. I am more sophisticated.
I want to know what I am paying for
and what I am getting.
I can by-pass the traditional
only-game-in-town suppliers.
I am less swayed by marketing gimmickry.
I am more selective.
I have competitive options.

The Changing Client!

Our business culture today is bottom line-sensitive. Everybody wants to know what they are receiving in return for what they are paying. Earlier we described the characteristics of the changing client. When it comes to making a decision based on your value, your prospects are probably thinking the following thoughts:

• How much money do you want me to invest?
• What type of return will I get on this investment?
• What type of results can I expect?
• You want me to pay you a fee—for what? A plan? Advice?
• What is the totality of your value package?
• How will these services align with my goals?
• What's the real value?
• Why should I do business with you?

These questions illustrate why we need to be truly consultative. Strategic questioning is required. You've got to feel as though you are playing chess, not checkers with your prospect. The game of checkers is transactional. It's usually one step at a time.

Most transactional people in the business, who I affectionately call, "registered vendors," sell like this. It drives me crazy when people are so short-termed in their focus. Registered vendors are just trying to sell products and are not listening to the fullest. Many clients have three to four registered vendors. But most serious clients have only one consultant: Someone who has earned that coveted distinction of trusted FE.

The concept of registered vendor should get you thinking: Are you perceived as a vendor or as a partner?

No More Vendor Parking Lots

Early in my sales career I remember driving to meetings and sales appointments, and parking in my prospect's parking lot. Can you visualize the vendor's spaces in the parking lot? To have some fun, (but I was serious) I would ask my clients, where do the partners park? Where is the partner's parking lot? I would always get a chuckle. They would get my point of wanting to be thought of (and treated) as a partner, not a vendor.

If you're positioning real value, acting like a strategic partner and earning the coveted distinction of trust, then you will be parking where the partners park. Another way to evaluate real value is by the impact you actually make on your clients. Let's take a look at another ladder now; one I call the Financial Entrepreneur Impact Ladder.

The Financial Entrepreneur
Impact Ladder™

The Financial Entrepreneur Impact Ladder depicts five different levels of selling/consulting behaviors. These selling/con-
sulting behaviors start at the lowest level and move upward.
They are defined as follows:

1. Mr. Nice Guy

This is also Mr. Hopeful. It's the individual who was "in the
neighborhood" and decided to stop by and say hello. He dis-
plays the temperament that everything is going great and that
he just wanted to see how you are doing. Time wasting is a
function of his behavior.

Another vendor term is "wholesalers." I encourage the money
managers and mutual fund companies reading this book to
eliminate this vendor connotation from your vocabularies. The
old paradigm of leaving brochures and promotional materials
for clients (got any golfballs?) needs to be replaced with an attitude of competing on value. Many forward-thinking services
firms have made this change. New titles, supported by updated

stories of distinction and offerings of value will begin the quest towards strategic partner status. This professional visitor and former coffee and doughnut guy needs to be re-invented.

2. Price/Performance Advisor

Have you ever competed on price before? Have you ever been challenged by a prospect to cut your fee to meet a competitor's pricing proposal? Yes, Mr. Ideal, my competitor said they would charge you what? Sure, I can beat that fee. Has that ever happened to you?

Or have you ever found yourself touting the performance of a money manager, a mutual fund or possibly your own recent or past success? If so, you are committing a deadly sin in this business. You should know that if you sell and live by performance, you die by performance. Obviously clients want good performance but it has to be positioned and represented correctly in the context of a long-term consultative plan.

Are you a price/performance advisor? Have you ever exhibited this behavior?

3. Technical Presenter

You're still parking in vendor parking lots if a lot of your time is spent as a technical presenter. This behavior is easy to spot when you are watching someone else in action. Who is doing all the talking? The good Lord gave you two ears and one mouth—which means you should be listening twice as much as you should be talking.

Technical presenters also often use language or technical jargon familiar only to themselves. Some like to show off that technical Wharton education or other industry license requirements. If you're being a technical presenter, before you know it, alphas, betas, standard deviation, efficient frontiers, net asset value, etc. are coming out of your mouth at machine gun pace.

You usually get a friendly look from your prospects unless they are technically trained as well. If this describes you, you need to follow the following adages:

• Try to understand before you are understood
• Be impressed before you become impressive
• Be interested before you become interesting
• Listen before you are listened to

Get the picture? The technical presenter is the ultimate "spray and pray" guy as well. He hears an opportunity to position or sell some of his services and starts pulling features and benefits out of his back pocket before the client even finishes her thought.

If you're at this stage, please, enough already with the mystery language and slow down. Connect emotionally and logically with your prospect. Don't overwhelm them with your mind. Let them overwhelm you with their long-term goals.

Have you ever exhibited the behavior of a technical presenter?

4. Need Satisfier

Finally, you're starting to move into that coveted partner area. As the title implies, you are entering a stage where you can start satisfying needs. The following behaviors define the "need satisfier":

• You realize why you have two ears and one mouth
• You are getting better at listening and responding to needs, but can still improve
• You are hearing opportunities that need further clarification that could be developed into needs
• You have an appreciation for the basics of consulting dialogue
• You usually ask good questions
• You position the features and benefits of your

157

products and services
- You know how to recognize some attitudes that your clients exhibit, and you can answer most questions well
- You sell in a fashion depicted as face-to-face, but you are starting to move your chair closer to your prospect's, respectfully and confidently
- You know how to request commitments
- You have an understanding of the sales cycle
- You know how to play checkers (transactional mode) and are learning how to play chess (strategic and highly consultative)

5. Strategic Partner

No more vendor parking lots at this level. You are inner circle quality. Your client appreciates your value, pays you for it and refers you passionately to others. This advocate wants to help you based on the help you have given them. The core behaviors of a world-class Financial Entrepreneur who is viewed as a high-level Strategic Partner are as follows:

Thinks and acts as an entrepreneur
You continually make investments to distinguish your organization/team/yourself.

Realizes that the most important thing they have to sell is themselves
You know how to position the value that your company provides and the value you provide through your solutions, but you realize they are buying you or your team and you that you are an expert.

Competes on value
You know it, you can price it, you can sell it.

Truly exhibits consultative behaviors
Black-belt consulting skills exhibited–your attitude/ knowledge/skills/tools are upper-level.

Earns the coveted distinction of trust
Trust defined: Total confidence that others have in three things that you possess: integrity, character and abilities. How many of your clients truly trust you?

Thinks and acts like a partner
You sit on the same side of the table with your client.

Exhibits conversational respect
You clarify, you confirm and you are masterful at acknowledging your clients' thoughts and statements (i.e., you make the emotional connection).

Can illustrate a process
You have a unique, comprehensive process–one that furthers your distinction.

Demonstrates unbelievable confidence
There is an aura about you–your prospect and client can feel it–they are thinking that this guy has his act together.

Passionate in all that they do and say
You love what you do and it shows.

No hesitation in response to critical questions
"Go ahead, make my day" is your attitude, and "ask me any question" is your mindset. Obviously, you do this at the highest levels of respect. There is no hesitation in your response.

So how would your clients rate you on this stepladder of behaviors?

Strategic Chess

I coach a lot of FEs who enjoy playing chess. A good player needs to think like a chess grandmaster, 10-20 moves ahead.

Like him, you should have that "sense" that a Bobby Fischer or Boris Spassky had in their heyday, strategically moving your pawns, rooks, bishops, knights, queen and king.

A good chess move is like consulting at its best. You're listening and processing your client's answers with respect. You see where the meeting needs to go. Your vernacular is smooth. Questions are flying. Your prospect wants more information on your background. You can discuss your UVP, and your business beliefs. Your file drawer in your virtual file cabinet is opening. Here is where the dialogue about your process is critical.

Client success is crucial at this point, so you open your umbrella of differentiation confidently, and YES you can now see this issue of real value entering the dialogue. However, in your game of chess both you and your clients win. The sales cycle moves forward and a partnership is in the making.

You're now deep into a dialogue with a prospect. If you win this business, it literally could make your year. Up to this point, you've done everything right. The sales process has been long and strategic. And just when you think you're at the end of this process and you're getting close to closure, the prospect looks at you and says in a nice, but challenging, way, "Why should I do business with you?"

When you hear those words, what are you thinking? Where does your mind go? How do you feel? More often than not, the nature of the question is challenging, even if a challenging tone is not used. This is a good time to reinforce everything you've been sharing with the prospect throughout the Value Ladder process. Do you feel you are ready to sum everything up, and that you will be confident in your delivery?

Now, how else might this question come up? Your prospect could say something like, "I'm not sure I have enough information to make a decision right now." There may still be some skepticism on his part. Maybe you haven't really connected yet.

160

Or it might be a genuine stall on his part. It's like the chess game–sometimes it just happens that neither player wins. Or maybe the prospect is still evaluating other alternatives and is having a tough time making a decision.

But remember (and how could you forget by now?), business is first a meeting of the hearts, and then it becomes a meeting of the minds. When you have emotionally and logically connected with your prospects, you have achieved the ultimate alignment of your value to theirs. It's important to understand that real value is achieved by qualitative means, and measured by quantitative means.

What does this mean? An example of a qualitative value is helping someone find their peace of mind. Maybe you're in an estate planning dialogue with prospects and you're discussing their legacy. Maybe there are charitable giving issues, goals to support the community more, or some intrinsic values that are important to that prospect. Perhaps they want to improve the quality of their life, or find an easier way to run their business which may have become too cumbersome and too tedious.

Quantitative value means making a logical connection–mind to mind. Your prospect may want an increase in his assets, for example, and gives you a half-million dollars for you to grow it to one million dollars. You develop an investment policy statement, allocate assets, monitor the managers and evaluate the performance–and you achieve his goal. That's quantitative value.

Many times, the achievement of quantitative value may lead to the achievement of what is in an individual's heart. Or, you might have dialogues with prospects on qualitative issues first (heart to heart) then map out a plan to achieve the quantitative–or logical–goals (mind to mind).

Maybe you've helped an organization increase their revenues. Perhaps the money manager you are working with was able to help your prospect's endowment or corporate retirement plan. If you help an institution reduce its fiduciary liability, well, that's a huge value for an ERISA plan.

These are just a few quantitative examples of value. Take a look at the list below which lists examples of both qualitative and quantitative real value. It will help give you ideas where you might provide more real value to your own prospects and clients.

You Should Do Business With Me Because I Can Help You Achieve This Type of Real Value:

Qualitative	Quantitative
• Peace of mind	• Increase assets
• Achieving a legacy	• Increase revenues
• Community support	• Increase assets under mgmt.
• Charitable endeavors	• Increase certainty of ROI
• Quality of life	• Accelerate cash flow
• Demonstrate ease of doing business	• Protect assets
• Confidence	• Reduce risk
• Loyalty	• Reduce costs
	• Reduce fiduciary liability

Net It All Out: What's the Bottom Line?

Prospects are now at the point where they want you to give them a summary of your presentation–a concise reason why they should do business with you. This is your chance to connect your unique value back to them, based on what they have shared with you.

The tangible examples of successes you've had with other clients will help you here. This, added to what you have learned from your current prospects, should tell them without a doubt, how you can help achieve their goals. A dialogue may sound like this:

162

Challenging Prospect (Mr. and Mrs. Ideal): "You've presented a compelling case for consideration. One final question, why should we do business with you?" (Big gulp) You start to go backward in your chair, possibly have some winging it thoughts. Time out. Rewind. That was the person you were *before* you started reading this book.

Now, you are in a relaxed position. A smile in your stomach begins. You take on an athletic posture. Now you feel like you are going forward in your chair. You feel you have world-class confidence, passion and speed. The new and improved FE's response might sound like this:

FE: (Long version) "Thank you, Mr. and Mrs. Ideal. I appreciate your interest and the possibility to partner with you. It would be a privilege to have you both as clients and I truly value the opportunity." (Now there's an emotional connector.) You continue, "We've discussed your key long-term wealth management goals. You have major issues to contend with in the broad areas of estate planning, retirement and income protection. You also have key issues regarding your children and your parents."

"Earlier I presented my team's UVP to you. That was our proposal of value. We're experts in what you are seeking. You should have a sense of our business beliefs and, most importantly, the process we will employ going forward to meet your goals. We've also shared client experiences that reflect your goals, showing you how we've helped them to achieve theirs. Hopefully you are comfortable with how we've differentiated our company and our solutions and our team."

"The real value will be in the results we'll be able to produce for you. Similar to the results we've achieved for others, we can save you money and put this plan into action to help you increase the certainty of achieving your total wealth management goals."

"As I mentioned earlier we value the opportunity to strategically partner with you. May we begin that opportunity now?"

- OR -

FE: (Short version) "Because we can provide real value to you, we can help you to achieve your goals. We've demonstrated it for others and we can do it for you. But you need to be comfortable with what we bring to the table—what our value is and how it aligns to what you've shared with us. The bottom line is that we truly believe we can help you achieve your goals. We have the expertise and the specialization you are seeking. We have demonstrated it for others, and we can do it for you."

The bottom line is that you can't talk like this unless you genuinely know what you're doing, have applied your value to others, and have helped others to achieve their goals. Then your value becomes real.

Financial Malpractice

Are you wondering if this question, "Why Should I Do Business With You?" will come up early in the dialogue before you've been able to answer the other six critical questions? My experience shows that it usually does not. Think about this. Why should a prospect ask *why* he should do business with you, if he never got around to first asking *what* you do?

If it does come up early in the dialogue, I might say something like, "Well, there are many reasons why I believe you should hire me, but I'm not sure yet if we're the right fit for each other. It's important to me that I have a good understanding of what you are looking for, and what you value, and that what I am capable of providing is in line with what you are looking for in a strategic partner."

Answering this question prematurely would be like a doctor prescribing a medication for an illness before he even runs tests and determines a diagnosis. It's what I call financial malpractice.

From Internal to External AHA!

When your work is accepted and applied, and your prospects accomplish goals due to the alignment of your value to theirs, then it all becomes real to them. If not, then it's all just a big claim. When I used to teach how to handle skepticism during my early days at the former Xerox Learning Systems, I explained that skepticism is simply doubt: prospects doubted your ability or your services. Maybe that point of doubt may surface with some of your prospects. But, as a world-class FE, you can't have doubt.

An organization, a team, or an individual all need to show examples of real value. Remember, real value is not the same as your UVP. **Real value is the application of your unique value in a customized way to prospective clients.** It's showing that you have provided results.

For final review: The UVP tells our prospects and clients what we do, but the UVP needs to be applied. When you develop custom applications or solutions for your clients, you suddenly realize you are creating "aha's" for yourself and for your clients. Your own "aha's" must first come from within. How can you expect someone else to connect with you if you don't feel this way inside yourself? That's your inner glow. If this isn't oozing out of your heart and your soul, how do you really expect to make that connection emotionally and logically with someone else? How can they feel it if you don't feel it?

When you come to grips with the fact that you provide value, and that you can bring your proposal of value alive for prospects in a way that will help them to achieve their big-picture goals, then it becomes real. And that, in essence, is the big "AHA" for your clients.

Strategic Questions to Consider

• How do you usually respond to the seventh Value Ladder question, "Why Should I Do Business With You?"
• How does your team respond to this same question?
• How do you define the real value you provide to your clients?
• Have you ever asked what your real value has been to them?
• How would your clients define the real value you provide?
• Do you consistently ask your clients how they will measure your success?
• Are you currently measuring the real value you offer?
• How are you documenting it?

Understanding your real value is key. This is an important concept for you to master. It requires continued introspection, quality dialogue with your existing clients, and asking for honest feedback on the value you've provided.

Questioning your existing clients will give you greater understanding. You'll learn about areas you can improve, to ensure you are on the path to providing real value. If you are providing real value, you increase the certainty of establishing a client for a lifetime. These are clients that you covet, clients whose values and appreciation and acceptance of your real value is understood and shared with future prospects. Isn't that what we all want?

Case closed.

You should be as exhilarated as Steve and I were when we reached the top of the mountain now that you've climbed to the top rung of the Value Ladder. You're at the top of your own mountain.

Congratulations!

$\Big($ Let's review the Value Ladder. $\Big)$

mirror mirror on the wall

am **i** the most valued

of them all?

Value Ladder™ in Review

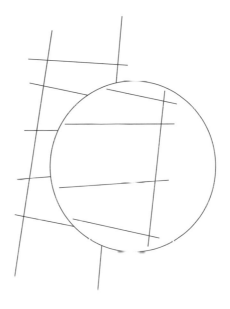

Value Ladder™ in Review

Climb high, climb far
Your goal, the sky,
Your aim, the stars.

– Anonymous

The climb up the Value Ladder certainly has been high and far. Shooting for the sky and aiming for the stars is a worthy goal– and is the attitude of many of the exceptional professionals I have had the privilege of partnering with over the years. By going from good…to great…to extraordinary…then eventually becoming the best you can be is what aiming for the stars is all about.

By now, you've learned a lot through the Value Ladder process. But before we address advanced applications, cultural issues and what you need to act upon, let's re-visit some of the key points you've learned so far:

- We are in the midst of a value revolution
- I have an improved understanding of the concepts of competing on value
- My clients are changing, have greater options, and are demanding custom solutions
- Our business has become commoditized
- I realize that first impressions happen only once, and that improving my answers to background questions will help me make a good first impression
- I have learned techniques for introspection and the creation of my Unique Value Proposition (UVP)
- I can identify my core business beliefs and philosophies regarding the solutions that I represent to others
- I can define my unique process, an important element to dis-

tinguish myself, by how I partner with clients to achieve their goals
- I can analyze my client base, discuss retention and growth of my client base over a lifetime, and understand its value to me
- I can share client successes and solutions I have provided without betraying client confidentiality
- I can differentiate myself from my competition in three ways: through my organization, through my solutions and, most importantly, through myself
- I understand real value and how to measure it qualitatively and quantitatively
- I have learned that my Value Ladder is like a virtual file cabinet
- I can use my virtaul file cabinet instinctively, in the moment. It is a compelling seven-drawer cabinet that can be "opened and closed" anytime
- I can improve my ability to deliver my message with confidence, passion and speed—with no more winging it

Let's also revisit some key instructional design issues regarding the development of the Value Ladder:

1. The power of the model is in its **simplicity**. It's an easy model to understand and follow; it flows logically.

I teach it in a linear fashion. We start at the bottom and work our way up. This was done for a reason. Many clients do in fact ask questions in this order. If they don't, they are no doubt thinking about these questions in one form or another.

The additional power of the model is that it allows you to capture all of the key critical questions in a compelling, thoughtful way that will further prepare you to distinguish the most important thing you have to sell...YOU!

2. The Value Ladder is **flexible**. The real world dictates that you need to be in the moment. You need not only to be prepared, but to be flexible and fluid as well—realizing you may need to open a virtual file cabinet drawer at any given point in time throughout your dialogues with prospects.

For example, you are in a meeting with a prospect and he jumps right into asking questions about your process immediately after you've answered the first question, "Who are you?" In other words, your prospect has leaped from question one to question four on the Value Ladder. Don't feel handcuffed. You can't say, "Well, that's a good question, but I need to tell you more about who I am, what I do, and why I do it, and then I'll be happy to answer how I do it."

Instead, you need to realize that in answering Value Ladder questions, you can go from step one to step seven to step four back to step two. You can go all over the map. But, usually there is a logical sequence to the questions prospects will ask, and then they just flow naturally.

Remember to stay in the moment. Even if the prospect poses questions out of order, be sure to be specific in answering each Value Ladder question they might ask. Stay on that rung of the Value Ladder with them for a minute. You will surely demonstrate conversational respect and improve your ability to connect emotionally. Your intuition will guide you where to move next.

The Value Ladder will help you stay in control. You are not a robot. This is not a mechanical process; you should be flexible as well.

3. The Value Ladder was built for a total **consultative** approach. Changing clients talk out of both sides of their mouths. One side says, "Do you really know what I value? Ask me questions, listen intently to me, be respectful, find out what's important to me."

But, be prepared—out of the other side of their mouth they want to know what your value is. They want to know how it aligns to what they value. We referenced sales trainer and author Mack Hanan earlier in the book who stated "You have to know your value before you can sell your value." Always remember that adage because it's a powerful one.

We also discussed the strategy of a chess games. A high-level strategic model of questioning called the "Value Questioning Strategy™" is a process we teach in our programs. It's in the mode of strategic chess. It supports the thesis that the good Lord gave us two ears and one mouth, and that we should be listening twice as much as we should be talking! We don't teach this concept in the Value Ladder process, though. Why? Because the Value Ladder is about discovering or knowing your value. Strategic questioning is part of the process of delivering your value or selling your value. It's a big distinction that needs to be understood.

When you become world-class in answering these questions, you'll find that your level of questioning, the confidence you express, and the ability to pull information out of your virtual file cabinet, will take you to higher levels of dialogue that you may never have otherwise reached.

Again, you have to know your value before you sell your value.

4. Although the Value Ladder is taught in a linear fashion, your final answers are best developed when you use your virtual screwdriver and **tighten up** previous steps after you learn a new one.

When my father taught me to change a tire, he showed me how to tighten each lug nut slowly to get support of the wheel and then to go back and make sure each lug nut was on tight enough. The same principal applies to the Value Ladder. You should work on your Unique Value Proposition, then go back and tighten your "background" screws a little more. Then, after you work on your business beliefs, come back and tighten your UVP and background screws. Repeat the process as you continue your climb.

Your Value Ladder answers will get tighter and tighter. They'll fit so well that, like a good set of tires that are in total balance, you'll feel the same with the compelling story of your business– tight, in balance and providing a world-class ride for your prospects.

5. Memorize the Value Ladder. I mean really get it down. Like a good actress or actor memorizing their lines, you can play the role at levels you might not have imagined. Athletes and other star performers get their routines down so well. We're wowed by their performances, but never fully appreciate the time and effort that go into the quest for excellence.

The best way to memorize the Value Ladder was proposed by a participant in a Michigan program. "Who, what, why, how…who what why", he offered. My first remark was, "*Excuse* me?" I didn't know where he was going with this comment. He explained, "These are the first words of each question going up the Value Ladder and it's a great way to remember it and utilize it." Just start at the bottom with "who are you" and climb up.

> **Why** should I do business with you?
> **What** makes you different?
> **Who** have you done it for?
> **How** do you do what you do?
> **Why** do you do what you do?
> **What** do you do?
> **Who** are you?

Try applying the Cumbayah song with those words. Who-What-Why-How…Who-What-Why. Sing it out as I do with participants. Have some fun learning the process. You'll always remember it.

174

6. Internalize your responses. You've got to get your answers down so well it will seem like you're preparing for the biggest test of your life. The class you've signed up for is called "Discovering Your Value" and your professor will be quizzing you with questions to the most compelling story you'll ever need to provide a prospect or client: The story of you, your business, and the value you provide.

Remember the time and effort you put into some of those high school and college tests, how important it was for you to ace that big exam, to get your average up and to stand out in the crowd with various designations like the National Honor Society, Magna Cum Laude, or Summa Cum Laude? It takes a lot of time to "get to great."

How much time do star performers invest to truly become world-class? In past programs, I've worked with an olympian, several former professional athletes, and an army ranger. I've talked to them about commitment and I've gotten some passionate responses. Are you good, great, extraordinary, or operating near full throttle of greatness?

Some of my participants performing at that level know exactly what I'm talking about. You make the call. How much more can you improve your ability to stand out in the crowd?

7. Remember to **personalize** your responses. This is where you begin to further separate yourself from other FEs in a prospect's pile of business cards. You should have one set of answers for all seven Value Ladder questions, but learning how to make them come alive for various people is a real art. For instance, I believe you need one Unique Value Proposition for your business. You can make it come alive to many different people. Be in the moment. Be flexible in your presentation, and be confident in your delivery.

Some participants have said, "Leo, I have multiple targets. I focus on retirees, widows and small business owners." That's okay. One UVP will suffice. Rehearse your conversations and you will see the flow starting to occur.

My conversation with a senior executive of a major Wall Street financial services firm may go something like this: They'll ask, "So, what do you do, Leo?" I say, "We specialize and partner with firms like yours to help your financial advisors distinguish themselves from your core competitors. We help them to keep and grow their existing business and to get more business by truly learning how to compete on the value they provide."

Next meeting is an hour later with a divisional manager from the same Wall Street financial services firm. Again the question is posed, "So, what do you do, Leo?" I then say, " We specialize and partner with firms like yours to help your financial advisors further distinguish themselves from their core competitors. We also can help your branch managers go through a process to learn how to distinguish their branches and become a branch of choice. We teach them to further understand how to deliver their value more effectively within their branches, and we train and coach the advisors in their branch to ultimately compete on the value they provide."

And last, but not least, I find myself at the same Wall Street financial services firm, now in conference with a group of their financial consultants. They ask, "So what do you do, Leo?" And I say, "I help committed, dedicated, serious financial consultants like yourselves to discover your value and teach you how to articulate it...with increased confidence, passion and speed."

Three different scenarios with the same company, but I needed to answer the question regarding my uniqueness on three different levels. All of the answers flow out of my one Unique Value Proposition. You simply need to know how to make your UVP come alive to the various people with whom you come in contact.

Like Investing, Communicating is Both an Art and a Science

Many portfolio managers over the years have told me that managing portfolios is both an art and a science. I believe what they're saying, in other words, is that they need to make decisions with both their hearts and their heads. Just like the money managers, you have to communicate to your coveted prospects and clients in the same way. Think. Be in the moment. Be flexible.

A part of you needs to be like a mad scientist who has created the perfect formula for the marketplace. Get your answers down with excellence. Just make sure you apply the creative and artistic touch, both in writing and more importantly, when verbalizing to truly stand out from the crowd.

Next, let's analyze some Value Ladder applications.

$$\Big(\ \text{Now is the time to wow your prospects.}\ \Big)$$

mirror mirror on the wall

am **i** the most valued

of them all?

CHAPTER ELEVEN

Advanced Applications for Your Value Ladder™

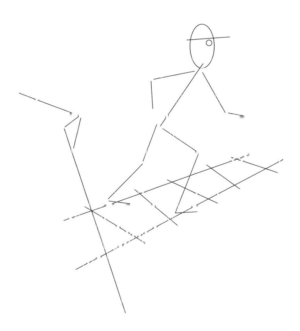

Advanced Applications for Your Value Ladder™

> *He who knows not, and knows not*
> *that he knows not, is a fool...shun him;*
> *He who knows not, and knows*
> *that he knows not, is ignorant...teach him;*
> *He who knows, and knows not*
> *that he knows, is asleep...wake him;*
> *But he who knows, and knows*
> *that he knows, is a wise man...follow him.*

– Ancient Proverb

I proudly tell those who ask about my background that I feel I received my theoretical doctorate in selling by working for the former Xerox Learning Systems. What a great time in my life! Imagine being paid to learn the business of selling, the business of consulting, and to help other major sales organizations do the same thing.

I loved my job and the people I worked with. So many times clients would kiddingly say, "You're not too excited about what you're selling, are you Leo?" I would laugh then, as I do today, when people ask the same question because I remain equallly excited. When was the last time someone said that to you? When was the last time someone said, "I see that you really love your work," or, "I can feel your passion for what you do." I believe those kind words say everything.

One of the great aha's for me in my sales training career occurred as I was helping and observing other sales professionals change their behaviors. We used to tout a four-step process for learning:

1. You have to acquire a new skill
2. You have to practice it
3. You have to transfer it
4. You have to apply it

And that's the challenge: The application of your new skills to the real world. Now we're talking business! To reach its highest level of validation, this application needs to achieve results. In your case, it might be increased assets or improved profitability, fewer clients, improved quality of life, and so on.

Sound familiar? Sound like real value? You have to be able to apply in order to achieve. Remember your UVP, your proposition of value? Remember your effort to find your real value? It's the *application* of your UVP to achieve those goals, qualitative and quantitative.

There are numerous applications that make your Value Ladder come alive. We will talk about six specific examples and illustrate unique applications to give you a greater sense of the flexibility of the entire model. Remember, the power of the model is in its simplicity. It's an easy model to understand and follow; it flows logically.

The First Application:
It's Alive! What the Value Ladder™ Sounds Like in Action

The following client dialogue illustrates how to use the steps of the Value Ladder effectively. This is a long version, but it can be used confidently with a prospect:

"Mr. Ideal, I'd really like to thank you for seeing me today. And I'd like to be sensitive to the time you've allotted for our meeting. After reviewing your objectives, I have developed an agenda and some core, critical questions. I would first like to review with you **who** I am, as well as provide some personal and professional background to give you a better perspective."

"The second area that I would like to focus on, Mr. Ideal, is **what** I do. I've developed a compelling and unique value proposition. It's a statement that aligns my value to what I believe might be the areas you are interested in. I am really proud of it."

"Third, I'd like to tell you **why** I do what I do. I have five core business beliefs of how I do business (invest funds, partner with clients). I'd like to spend some time with you to review these beliefs."

"The fourth area, Mr. Ideal, is **how** I work with individuals or groups like yourself. I have a very comprehensive five-step process. And I'll be happy to illustrate this process for you."

"The fifth step in my presentation will give you a better sense of **who** I have done this for. I've had tremendous client success, and since I specialize in targeting individuals like yourself, I'd like to share with you some of my clients' broader parameters and how I've been able to align my unique value to their needs."

"My sixth step is **what** makes me different. Mr. Ideal, my clients want to know how our organization is different, and how our solutions are different. I truly believe that the most important business decision you will ever make is whether you want to sit on the same side of the table with my team and me. I am prepared to talk more about what we stand for individually, and what you should expect from partnering with us."

"Last of all, Mr. Ideal, and perhaps the most important questions you may want answered, is **why** you should consider doing business with us. What's the real value we provide? What do we bring to the table, and how do we connect to the things you value?"

"I am prepared to walk you through this process. Is this in line with the expectations you have for the time we'll be spending together today? Are there any other issues I should be aware of?"

The Second Application:
A Shorter Dialogue for You

Now you have a good idea of how flexible the Value Ladder can be in any client/prospect situation. But, let's say you have a limited time in your prospect's office. If you only have about 30 minutes, the following dialogue makes a concise use of the time, and gets your message across succinctly and confidently.

You want to make sure you give the best impression and hit all the points on the Value Ladder in whatever time you have. Okay, here's how you can do it without sounding like that guy in the old FedEx commercial (who talked so fast that no one understood him) and still address the seven questions:

"Mr. Ideal, I really appreciate your time today; and I'd like to be sensitive to the half hour you've given me so why don't I spend a little time sharing with you who I am, and explaining what my unique value is, followed by outlining my five business beliefs. These beliefs are supported by a very comprehensive five-step process. I've spent a lot of time on this and I truly believe every step is differentiable, and I'd like to walk you through it."

"I'd also like to share with you a little bit about the clients we work with. You are exactly like one of our typical clients, and I'll give you some examples of our successes. I'll spend some time distinguishing my company, our solutions, and why you should consider partnering with my team and me. I'd like you to understand the real value behind what we do, and what we can do to align our expertise to help you accomplish your goals. Now, is that in line with what your expectations for our time today? Is there anything else I should be sensitive to?"

Third Application:
The Value Ladder™ is a Sales Opportunity Tool for You

The Value Ladder comes alive even further when you start applying your strategic and consultative questioning skills along with the proper emotional connection skills. In your questioning process there will be areas (or folders) in your virtual file cabinet that you can selectively pull out to connect with whomever you may talk to.

For example, a prospect might say, "I have a 20-year horizon, and I don't want to get caught up in some flashy, quick-hit investment. That's what's important to me." You might respond to the prospect, "Well, Mr. Ideal, tell me more about that. Did you have a bad experience in the past, or have you been in a negative situation, or is this just a philosophy you have?" Go deeper. Acknowledge. Clarify. Confirm.

Most FEs might not ask a prospect a question quite like that. Instead, they may say, "You're right, and I am in this for the long term for you, as well." But if you responded the first way, you could go into your file drawer #3 with your business beliefs which state that you believe an investor must have a customized investment policy statement, and that they need to think long-term about their financial planning.

So you would then say, "Mr. Ideal, when you mentioned your time horizon and not wanting some quick-hit investment, that totally aligns with one of my core business beliefs. I've learned this is in my own business as well."

Unfortunately, some FEs throw all of their products, services, and features against the wall and hope something sticks. They "spray and pray." They are not even thinking clearly about positioning their seamless, integrated solutions. Or they "tell versus sell" just like the Technical Presenter on our FE Impact Ladder who does all the talking. If you find yourself slipping into this mode, remember that you should be consulting and asking the critical questions, responding and linking the conversation back to your unique message on the Value Ladder.

As a result of your world-class listening skills, your prospect will talk more. Look for opportunities to pull manila folders out of your virtual file cabinet. Use them wisely. After all, they should contain everything you need to answer any Value Ladder question.

Fourth Application:
The Value Ladder™ Questioning Model

Another creative application for the Value Ladder is to use it in reverse, as a potential probing model for your clients. For example, if you are meeting with a million-dollar-plus prospect, for instance, a business owner or a corporate executive, you might say something like, "Thank you for taking the time to talk to me today. Last week on the phone, you mentioned you had some questions for me. And I'm prepared to answer them. One of the most comprehensive processes I use helps explain who I am, what I do, why I do it, how I partner with people like yourself, who else I work with, and what makes me different. It also includes why you might want to consider working with me."

"At the same time, I'd like to ask you a few questions as well, Mr. Ideal. I'd like to know more about you and your background." (This sounds like Value Ladder question number one in reverse, doesn't it?)

"I'd also like to know more about the value you provide to some of your own clients in your business, Mr. Ideal." (Hmmm…sounds like Value Ladder question number two, doesn't it?)

"What are some of the business beliefs that drive the strategies for your business?" (Gee, sounds like Value Ladder question number three.)

"Can you tell me about the process you use to partner with your clients, to give me a better understanding of your success and how you work?" (Hmmm…sounds like Value Ladder question number four to me.)

"And, Mr. Ideal, who might be some of your typical clients? Give me a better sense of the individuals you work with so I can understand your organization better. This helps me better position my work." (This sounds like Value Ladder question number five.)

"Can you please tell me how you distinguish your company from your core competitors? How do you separate yourself from the crowd in your industry?" (Sounds like question number six.)

"Finally, in your business, what is the real value you provide to your clients, Mr. Ideal?" (Wow, real value comes alive even when you ask clients these questions.)

See how powerful this application can be? Just remember to be conversational and respectful with your approach. Don't ask questions in rapid-fire succession. Take your time, slow down, and you will be surprised at what you will discover. I've known many FEs who successfully use this model. The prospects are very impressed with the professionalism of the approach, and with the thoroughness of the questions.

Fifth Application:
Use the First Three Questions to Determine Compatibility

When you look at the first three questions of the Value Ladder, you'll see how powerful they really are. They provide a great method for understanding your prospect's background, unique value to others, and to determine what type of FE that prospect is looking for. This is when you ascertain the chemistry between the two of you.

You could spend your entire first meeting with a prospect on these three questions. If there is a disconnect with a prospect at this point on the Value Ladder, most likely incompatibility will force you to move on to the next prospect.

Many times, the first meeting is one of mutual interviewing. The prospect needs to interview you. At the same time, you need to interview the prospect. If you sense compatibility based on the answers to the first three questions, then you have a solid reason to establish a second meeting where you can go deeper into your process and answer other higher Value Ladder questions.

Sixth Application:
Competitive Evaluation Tool for High-Level Prospects

Turn the Value Ladder over to your prospect! This tool is used to help you in a competitive situation. The prospect can use it to help discern your value from your competitor's. You are, in essence, handing over the seven Value Ladder questions to a prospect and suggesting they use them as a "probing model" in discussions with other prospective FEs.

A word of caution though: You'd better be black-belt with your own answers before you consider this Value Ladder application.

If you are at the point in your presentation where you ask the prospect where you stand in terms of what and who they are evaluating, and they say, "I'm talking to another FE from a large, reputable firm." You might respond, "That's great. Help me to understand your situation better—in which stage are you in this evaluation process? How are you going to make your decision, and which criteria will you use?"

As I mentioned before, if you know for certain that you are in a very competitive scenario, try the following statement. You may see the risks, but I think it shows unbelievable confidence—here's what I would say to your prospect, "Maybe I can add more value to you in your decision process. Write these seven questions down, Mr. Ideal, and ask them of the other firm or FE you are interviewing."

Then say to your prospect, "If I were in your shoes, having to make an important decision like this, these are the seven questions I would ask in order to make my decision. You should receive nothing less than black-belt answers because you are making a big decision for your future. And if you haven't asked these questions, you need to, Mr. Ideal. You need to respectfully challenge us (FE's) because we need to enhance your comfort level with our value before we earn the right to partner with you. This way you are more informed and make the best possible decision."

This is a powerful approach. It's important for you, as a financial entrepreneur, to not only ask the right questions, but also to help your prospect ask them. Remember, you shouldn't try this approach unless you have your own world-class answers down pat, and can deliver them with confidence, passion and speed.

Remember Mark Colgan, the FE whose life had changed literally overnight with the death of his wife? In Mark's newly created brochure he adapted this concept of educating clients. He took the idea of the seven Value Ladder questions and created his own reverse model to properly educate some of his key prospects and help them with their own advisor selection process. Here is Mark's list for your review:

Seven Questions to Ask a Potential Financial Advisor

1. Who is this advisor? What are this financial advisor's credentials and experience?

2. What does this particular financial advisor do? What services does this person provide, including specialized services?

3. What is the advisor's philosophy? What are his or her core beliefs and principles regarding money management?

4. How does this financial advisor accomplish his or her goals? How does this financial advisor implement solutions (the process often being more important than the solution itself) and is the process unique?

5. Who is this financial advisor's clientele? Who are the financial advisor's clients, and are testimonials provided?

6. Does anything distinguish this advisor from the others? Are this person's services different or unique vis-à-vis others' services?

7. How will using this particular advisor benefit me? What real value does he or she bring to the table and how will it improve my life?

I know it would impress the heck out of me if someone presented their approach with authority and respect like Mark did with his list. I would know I was dealing with a professional who really had her act together.

The Last Word

It never fails that after my presentations FEs come up to me and ask, "Leo, how do you get to the point where the words just flow from your mouth like they do? How can I get to the point where I am eloquent and articulate in all my presentations? It seems so easy for you."

Well, I give the same answer every time I'm asked: What I do is no different from what YOU do every day. I just rehearse my presentation over and over. I do it consistently, and I make a conscious effort to make it sound the same all of the time. That way I have the basics down, and I can add or subtract from my presentation depending upon the particular circumstances. It is now in my soul, in my blood, in my veins. This is what will make the message compelling too. You have to "practice what you preach." You have to embody it. You have to apply it.

When you learn to deliver your answers to the seven critical questions on the Value Ladder with confidence, passion and speed, you and your message will become so conversationally compelling that your attitude will be, **"Why wouldn't this prospect want to do business with me?"**

Susan Burton, president of Susan K. Burton and Associates, Inc., is a great friend and strategic partner of our firm. Back in the mid-'90s, Susan held a decision-making position with a major Fortune-500 organization that was considering my firm for a major training initiative. We had a meeting, and afterward in a final comment, I said to Susan with utmost sincerity, "Why wouldn't you want to do business with us?" I meant it from the bottom of my heart and she knew it.

Susan smiled when I asked her that question, and still smiles today when she tells that story. We reminisce occasionally and laugh about that memorable dialogue. In retrospect, it was a precursor to some interesting analysis and decisions that eventually led to the development of our strategy, and a new strategic partner.

This is another example of practicing what you preach, feeling so strongly about what you do that you can say something like this with respect and sincerity. When you apply your knowledge and skills, you'll be amazed at the results you will see.

$\Big($ Ready to develop a culture of value? $\Big)$

mirror mirror on the wall

am **i** the most valued

of them all?

CHAPTER TWELVE

Creating a Culture of Value

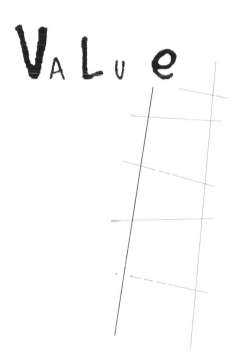

Creating a Culture of Value

> *Culture Counts...*
> *An organization that truly believes in*
> *maximizing intellect can't have multiple cultures.*
>
> – Jack Welch,
> *JACK...Straight From The Gut*

Culture begins with an attitude and requires a mighty effort. Arguably, Jack Welch, former CEO of General Electric, is as qualified as anyone to teach this subject. As implied in the quote above from his recent autobiography, you'd better all be singing from the same hymnal to effect change, and to achieve the goals important to your organization.

It's true that there is a correct way to create a culture. It's not only articulated from the top, but also practiced at the top. As the president and CEO of your organization (whether a large firm or a small team), you should have completed your Value Ladder and everybody–I mean everybody–who is involved with your clients should, as well.

Anyone in this chain should be able to demonstrate confidence, passion and speed. Anyone can understand the value they provide. No if's or but's. But some don't really live it. Some organizational preachers are simply that: Preachers. Do as I say; not as I do. They don't practice what they preach and are similar to the changing client we've mentioned throughout the book–they talk out of both sides of their mouth.

It's a new world for business. Remember the old days when quality was an afterthought? Consumers finally gave American companies a financial slap aside the head and shouted,

"HELLO? We want excellent products at a fair price. Provide them or we'll go elsewhere for satisfaction." So they flocked to less expensive, better-made imports. Quality became king.

The message came through loud and clear.

During the quality craze of the '80s, every business publication, business leader, and sales professional cried out for the need to focus on internal quality. Quality initiatives, quality teams, quality circles, total quality management, and quality processes sprang up everywhere. Winning organizations made the demand for quality integral to every person, process and product they pushed through their doors. Quality became so important that Congress even authorized the creation of the Malcolm Baldrige National Quality Award.

The reason quality interventions are so successful in some companies—the type that have won the awards, for example—is because the chairman and CEO have embraced quality initiatives and then the attitude trickles down. Organizations need a Jack Welch-type focus and commitment to put it all into place and have everyone working in sync. The only significant difference in the individual-vs-team-vs-branch-vs-division-vs-corporate culture is the directional guidance, traits and qualities of the leader. It's not a "Do-as-I-say, not-as-I-do" type of mentality that creates success. That's where companies run into problems.

Similarly, if you truly believe we still are in the midst of a value revolution and that clients are continuing to change, then where does that lead you? Your culture. What could be more important than that? What is keeping you from evaluating this pressing task at hand?

Creating a New Culture for Organizations: The Process is Top-Down

When I offered training for Fortune 500 companies in the 80s, the commitments at the organizational level started with the leaders–the CEOs–then trickled down to VPs of sales and marketing, national sales managers, national marketing directors, regional directors and finally right down to the sales force.

Now, consider the organizational structure at the typical financial services firms. What is the difference in their respective sales methods and messages? And why is one culture easier to create than the other?

The difference is that sales reps at Kodak, Bausch and Lomb or Xerox sold the same things over and over, i.e., film, contact lenses, copiers, etc. They had the same message. In our business of financial entrepreneurs, however, individuals have their own unique value and a set of beliefs delivered in their own unique ways.

Most times, FEs choose their own entrepreneurial way to do business, and select the solutions they want to promote. Firms try to be advisor-sensitive, so creating a unified culture becomes very difficult. This is because the FE wants to protect the entrepreneurial nature of their business practice.

One of the key challenges of senior management teams is to create a culture with a group of financial entrepreneurs. If you are the head of an organization with one sales force and one unified message to convey, then that's what you have to do: create one unified, consistent, repeatable message for your marketplace. It's easier to manage and reinforce. Firms like Fidelity, Schwab, Rittenhouse or Phoenix Investment Partners, for example, should each have a single, consistent sales message that the entire sales organization espouses. They should proclaim their uniqueness to the marketplace.

If you are an individual practitioner working for a firm and are focusing heavily on your own and your team's unique story, you are presented with a different challenge than what large organizations face. Reinforcing a single culture among a group of individualistic entrepreneurs is difficult. But, it can be accomplished.

The Value Ladder is not the end-all, though. It's the chassis. It's the cornerstone, albeit seven separate stones. Creating a culture of value should include the seven steps listed below. Study the CULTURE list and then conduct your own value audit. This could be your value judgment day!

Creating a Culture of Value

Since creating a culture is a top-down approach, let's start at the top and break down the word 'culture' letter by letter, and analyze it carefully.

Challenge Yourself and Your Organization to Greatness

Understand Your Value Gaps and Act

Listen Aggressively to Your Clients

Total Commitment to the Initiative

Utilize All the Requisite Skills

Respectful Dialogue with All Involved

Enjoy the Ride and Measure Your Success

Now, let's explore each letter on the culture chain from the top down.

197

Challenge Yourself and Your Organization to Greatness. We began this book with references to people and organizations that are truly great. Is that what you want to be considered as by your clients?

- Is your vision so compelling that others in your organization get pumped just listening to you?
- What are you trying to become?
- How do you want to be known?

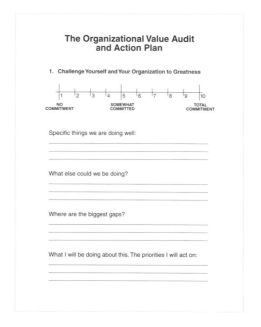

Stretch yourself with your thinking. Begin with the end in mind. Are you shooting the extra 100 foul shots a day, working on your short game to improve your golf scores, working out and sweating a little more to get in better shape?

The same principles apply here. Creating a culture of value requires living and working hard every day. By creating consistent, memorable experiences, clients will tell others how great you are. The key is to challenge everyone involved. You may surprise yourself in the process.

Understand the Value Gaps and Act

- Where are you now?
- Where do you want to go?
- Where is the gap?
- What strategies need to be employed?
- What are your priorities?
- What tactics do you act on?
- Do you want to develop a wealth management practice?
- Do you want to transition yourself to a fee-based practice?
- Remember all of those qualitative and quantitative examples of real value?
- What are you striving for?

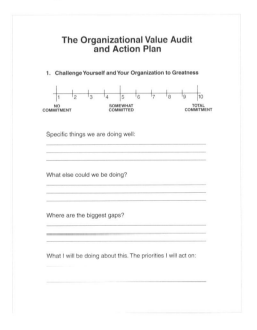

Start thinking and talking in terms of value goals. What's a value goal? Start with growth and retention of key clients. Develop your ideal client list with an emphasis on lifetime value. Assess what they value about you. Discover the gaps. Fill them in. Deliver more value. Grow the relationships you covet, then go after more ideal clients.

Listen Aggressively to Your Clients. I recently completed a business retreat with some of my key clients. One of our exercises was to define advice. What is this thing called advice? If this is one of the key ingredients all of you are competing against, then what, exactly, is it?

Many attributes were identified, but one in particular stood out: to listen aggressively. We talked about the word aggressive which, by dictionary definition, is "bold, combative and forceful." That truly is not respectful or consultative. Instead, the group defined their version of the word as more passionate with an emphasis on real listening, as in real value.

Maintain respect, but get into the heads of your clients by emphasizing the intent to understand even better. Your clients may be external or internal. Are you truly listening to them about the issues they value? Be honest. This is advanced acknowledgement, advanced clarification, advanced confirmation. Try it for yourself. It works. Listening skills at their highest levels will differentiate you from the competitors.

The Organizational Value Audit and Action Plan

3. Listen Aggressively to Your Clients

1	2	3	4	5	6	7	8	9	10

NO COMMITMENT   SOMEWHAT COMMITTED   TOTAL COMMITMENT

Specific things we are doing well:

_____
_____
_____

What else could we be doing?

_____
_____
_____

Where are the biggest gaps?

_____
_____
_____

What I will be doing about this. The priorities I will act on:

_____
_____
_____

Total Commitment to the Initiative. Some executives have said to me that they would like to extend the influence of our work in their firms. Extending the influence is one thing; creating a culture is another. To create a culture you have to lead. You have to be like Los Angeles Lakers coach Phil Jackson. You have to get on the horse and lead your team to battle. What can you, as the CEO of your team, be doing? How can senior executives start the process of creating a culture of value? Here's how: Help your organization by giving them the proper training. There must be a budget to help your organization compete at world-class levels based on your company's unique value. You should have value messages penetrate all communications inside and outside the company. Preach the message. Like a good branding strategy, include it on everything. It just makes good business sense.

The Organizational Value Audit and Action Plan

4. Total Commitment to the Initiative

```
+----+----+----+----+----+----+----+----+----+
1    2    3    4    5    6    7    8    9    10
NO             SOMEWHAT                 TOTAL
COMMITMENT     COMMITTED               COMMITMENT
```

Specific things we are doing well:

_____

_____

What else could we be doing?

_____

_____

Where are the biggest gaps?

_____

_____

What I will be doing about this. The priorities I will act on:

_____

_____

Utilize all the Requisite Skills. Reduce the pressure to function solely in the vendor mode and encourage working in a consultative mode. Are you at the top of the Financial Entrepreneur Impact Ladder we discussed in Chapter 9? Review it again. How are you consulting clients and being perceived? Be honest, and make the necessary behavioral changes. If you are committed, be prepared for a time and dollar investment to change. Again, are you simply interested, or are you committed? Mack Hanan said it best throughout the chapters of his book, *Competing on Value.* I have added my thoughts next to his chapter titles:

- Chapter One: Value Strategy–Do you have one? This is an investment policy statement for yourself–not for managing your investments, but for building a business around value.

- Chapter Two: Know Your Value–This is your Value Ladder to the fullest.

- Chapter Three: Price Your Value–You can't price it unless you know it. Do you have integrity in your pricing model? Can you articulate it with confidence, passion and speed?

- Chapter Four: Sell Your Value–These are your required consultative skill sets that reiterate your value.

- Chapter Five: Control Your Value–Retain and grow your clients. Again, **are you convinced that your clients are convinced that you add value?**

Respectful Dialogue With All Involved. There is no substitute for respect. But, there are ways to challenge respectfully. A meeting of the hearts connotes respect. My retreats are filled with coaching terms like, "Do it again, look me in the eyes, you can do better than that." The important element of a respectful challenge is the tone. You need to be a drill instructor. But, be conscious of respect, and you'll always have a willing listener and friend. Don't forget to initiate discussions with staff at all levels about knowing and communicating their value. Involve everyone who comes in contact with your clients. You'll be surprised how much it sinks in when you enter a strategic dialogue with all members of your team. You WILL learn. In a business of few guarantees, I can promise you that.

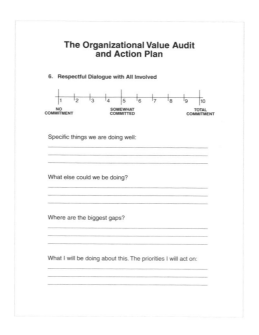

Enjoy the Ride and Measure Your Success. Life is too short to not have fun. Do what you love. Stop worrying. Find your value and articulate it to your ideal clients. They are out there waiting to be helped. And keep a scorecard. It's always more fun to track the goals you've achieved and to live your life to the fullest. So many people are doing it, why can't you? It's your choice and no one else's.

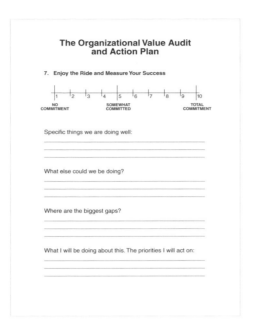

Are You a Value Zealot?

Some companies are listening to the value message. And these firms are becoming value zealots. I've had the privilege of working with senior management at a few of these companies, and it's exciting to see the transformation from old thinking to new. It's a transformation that many other firms–if they want to succeed–should emulate.

The secret to success, however, is not to view competing on value as a quick fix, sales gimmick or empty slogan. The pace-setting executives know that they must create a culture of value. They understand that before the company's sales and marketing representatives can begin talking about value to clients, value must become as pervasive as quality as a standard of performance for the entire organization. The savvy leaders are ensuring that their companies are "value ready" before approaching clients on value terms.

Relating to clients in terms of value, however, requires strategic positioning and thinking. At each level of the organization there must be a value audit. This is a serious, honest appraisal of whether or not the company is ready to begin articulating its value, and whether individuals at each level are properly prepared to do so.

Make your culture come alive. A typical audit will deepen your strategic thinking. It might look something like this:

Senior Management

- Is management totally committed (philosophically and financially) to helping the entire organization adopt a value mindset by creating a value culture?

- Do they view a value mindset as a necessary part of organizational life, equally as important as quality?

- Do they view selling or consulting based on the principles of value as a deeply ingrained element of their staffs, or just a short-term sales booster?

- Do they have a retention and growth strategy in place for their existing FEs so they can deliver ongoing value to meet the needs of their key producers?

Regional/Divisional/Branch Management

- Does management fully understand the value philosophy?

- Are they embracing the new value culture? If not, why not?

- Are they trained to coach others and reinforce the principles of competing on value?

- Do they have a mindset of becoming the regional/divisional/branch of choice for FEs they covet?

Financial Entrepreneurs

- Have you been through an introspective discovery process that helps you find the true value you provide?

- Have you internalized it strongly?

- Are you developing and using value-based strategies to distinguish yourself?

- Can you articulate your value and the company's value to clients?

Client Service and Support Staff

- Do the Client Service and Support Staff know the marketplace and their solutions inside out? More importantly, do they know their clients inside out?

- Do they understand the financial ramifications of keeping and growing the client base?

- Are they able to reinforce the value messages being communicated to clients by others in the company?

These are some introspective questions for all levels of management to consider.

The critical question that managers from top to bottom must answer is this: Are they prepared to do whatever it takes to alter their thinking so that they align their value to the client's value? If yes, they can become coveted, long-term partners with their clients. If no, they are doomed to the short-term, one-shot sales mentality. They will become registered vendors.

The value revolution has been around for a while and continues to be today's reality. Will you survive and prosper—or fail?

One Final Note on Commitment

If all you do is show up, say a few words about your commitment, and move on to your next organizational meeting, I seriously doubt your commitment. I'll bet if you surveyed all the winning CEOs of the The Malcolm Baldrige National Quality Award, you'd discover that they all were in the trenches with their troops. Here are a few of the winning service organizations over the years:

2000 – Operations Management International, Inc
1999 – The Ritz-Carlton Hotel Company
1997 – Merrill Lynch Credit Corporation
1996 – Dana Commercial Credit Corporation
1994 – GTE Directories Corporation
1992 – The Ritz-Carlton Hotel Company
1990 – Federal Express Corporation

Not only are they embracing the concepts they espoused, but they also are finding ways to improve them by teaching and mentoring others. You can do the same.

$\Big($ It's now time for action. $\Big)$

mirror mirror on the wall
am **i** the most valued
of them all?

What Are You Going To Act On?

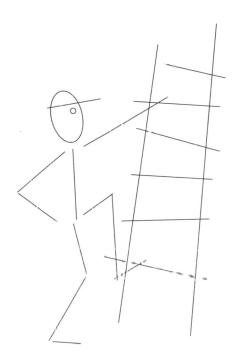

What Are You Going to Act On?

Vision without action is simply a dream
Action without vision just passes the time
Vision and action can change your world.

— Joel Arthur Barker

I enjoy telling the story about having to make some critical decisions about my career. I was having dinner at Gallagher's Steak House in New York City with a good friend, Bob Daugherty, currently a senior executive with Pricewaterhouse-Coopers. Bob is one of my closest friends, a college buddy, and he has a gift for getting to the root of real issues.

We discussed my career accomplishments so far, what my goals were, and the various ways I planned on reaching them. I told him I had some real business challenges and concerns. My seven emotional issues were fully in action. After dinner, as we walked back down the Avenue of the Americas, Bob said, "What did you get out of our discussion tonight, Leo?" I said, "Well, a lot of things." And I ran off a list of items that I needed to think about.

Bob was clearly getting frustrated with me as I continued to go down the list of things that needed to be done. He stopped me in my tracks, and, as only as a good friend could do, put his hand on my shoulder and literally put his finger in my face to make a strong point. He said, "Leo, I really don't care what you heard, I want to know what you are going to act on."

That really hit home with me. In essence, he was saying that I couldn't really effect change until I moved forward. I had to take action. All the words in the world couldn't help me accomplish my goals. I had to put them in motion.

Easier Said Than Done

Here's where you need to take that leap, take that risk, and be disciplined and motivated enough to make your move toward achieving your goals. As I've said throughout the book, it's not an easy process. It's demanding and challenging, which is what great learning and discovery processes are all about. They force you to think.

Dr. David S. Viscott said it best in his book, *Risking: How to Take Chances and Win,* "Before you can act, you must believe you need to change." He says it perfectly. "If you cannot take risk on your own behalf, you are not your own person. You are your biggest problem." As I have said—you, my friend, are your biggest competitor.

Another one of Dr. Viscott's quotes says it equally well, "If you cannot risk, you cannot grow. If you cannot grow, you cannot become your best. If you cannot become your best, you cannot be happy. If you cannot be happy, what else matters?" Wow!

We've talked a lot about going from good...to great...to extraordinary. To get to your destination, you must act. Before you can act, you must change. You must accept risk. So where do you go from here? Will you be flying, taking a train, renting a car, riding a bike, or taking a leisurely walk? How are you going to act?

Many have said, "You're either interested, or you're committed." If you are committed to going from good to great, from great to extraordinary, from extraordinary to the best possible person you're capable of becoming, then you MUST schedule the time with yourself to work on the most important thing you represent to others...YOU.

It's like starting the diet, beginning the exercise program, the golf lessons, learning Spanish—all the things you've always talked about doing: It's the coulda'-woulda'-shoulda'-type stuff. Think about it. You will put yourself through an intensive process of introspection and discovery, thinking in ways you've never thought before. You will push yourself to come up with answers that you've taken for granted for years. It's attitudinal; it's a realization that this process is very important and you need to act upon it right away.

If you believe as I do—that whatever it was that got you to this point is not good enough to get you to where you want to go tomorrow—then you must act! Here are some key thoughts on what you could act on. These thoughts, of course, assume you want to act, you're willing to change, and you're ready to risk.

The 7 Successful Keys to Action

1–Work on your personal Value Ladder™ as it exists today. Whatever it is, it is. No excuses. Just write down your answers. I'm looking for speed here. Even if you have an existing brochure, or you're thinking, "I've gone through a similar process just recently." It doesn't matter. Just start writing. I'm looking for an open attitude of improvement. Always, always, always, be honest. Are you good, are you great, are you extraordinary? Can you get better? Write on. If you are a member of a team, make sure each team member does the same thing. After all, don't you want to be singing from the same hymnal?

2–Schedule retreat time for yourself and/or your team. Find some time to truly work on your business. Begin quality strategy dialogue with your "friend in the mirror...YOU" or your team. Where are you going? What type of life do you want for yourself, your family? What type of compelling business model will you need to create, fix, or improve, to get that life? With the pace of change as fast as it is today, your business plan should be no longer than two years out. There's no harm in developing your dreams for the long term, but be realistic. Continue your strategic questions, "Who are your ideal clients? What do you want to be known for? What are you truly great at? What should you be doing more of in the future?" Couch these questions and answers beside your existing Value Ladder answers. Your aha's should continue to happen.

3–With a better understanding of your business and personal goals, get back to work on your improved Value Ladder™ answers. Where are the gaps? What do you feel really good about? What needs refinement in your story? Be tough on yourself. Push yourself. Visualize that I am your personal coach: 10 more push-ups–5 more–you can do it! Picture your Value Ladder screwdriver trying to tighten up your answers. Do it again. This time don't look at your notes. Eyeball- to-eyeball connections. That's it. Now, do it again. Repetition. Repetition. Repetition. Athletes do it. You should too, if you want to be the best you can be.

4–You need to be serious about creating a culture of value. Whether you are a sole practitioner, part of team, or a member of a larger organization, complete the Organizational Value Audit and Action Plan. This will give you more ideas on where you really stand on your commitment to compete on value and, more important, what you need to act on.

5–Re-visit your emotional issues. Yes, you do have challenges, circumstances, concerns, frustrations, needs, opportunities, and problems. Be honest. Be introspective. Dr. Viscott says, "True introspection is both self-critical and self-accepting. You seek to understand your answers and to find the origins of your feeling and attitudes." He continues, "You need to understand the events in your life. You need to know the role you play in your own difficulties. Unless you know how you stand in your own way, your best self will elude you. The fear of being introspective is the dread of finding a part of yourself you do not or cannot value. You can never become the true master of what is unknown to you until you make it known, and emotional pain will not go away until it is fully experienced. Besides, there are also many good points hidden by your defenses." Game. Set. Match. Remember, you have to know your value before you can price your value, and ultimately, sell it. Need I say more?

6–Go and visit–yes, visit–your clients. Start with your Top 10 ideal clients. Apply aggressive listening techniques. That's right. Don't just listen half-heartedly. Really listen carefully, and go deeper. Ask your clients, "What have we done well? How can we improve? Are there areas in which we haven't been as responsive as you'd like?" Don't ask for referrals now. Wow. Again, we are running contrary to popular opinion here. Don't worry about how your clients can help you right now. Just discover everything you can in order to help **them** more. If you can indeed help them more, the best quality referrals you will ever get will come directly from them without having to ask. In his final words before a surgery from which he never recovered, my dad told me, "Son, take of yourself and your family, take care of your business. I'll be okay." I urge you to take care of your business. That means, taking care of all your internal (colleagues, staff) and external (actual) clients. You'll be ok. Reconnecting with your clients will revalidate your value. It will also give you ideas on how to improve your proposition of value and your delivery of **real** value. Go for it.

7–Based on your new and improved Value Ladder™ answers, develop a branding strategy for your marketplace. From business cards to envelopes, from brochures to web sites, look for all the ways to proclaim your unique message to potential ideal clients. Assume an attitude of excellence. Whatever you do in your branding strategy, do it within your budget and your capabilities. If you believe that your best investment to suggest, the best stock story to tell, and the best thing to sell is you, then craft your strategy, apply your Value Ladder, and price your value correctly. The easiest thing for you to sell should be that competitor in your mirror...YOU!

There are only two more things to say: **Just do it!** Thank you, Nike. **Just act!** Thank you, Bob.

A Final Thought to Consider

In light of the rapid changes taking place in our industry and the challenges that lie ahead for financial entrepreneurs, competing on value holds tremendous power and potential for you.

I hope this book has been the beginning of your journey to discovering your value, that you already have some answers, and that you have experienced a few aha's as you have climbed the seven steps with me.

Stay focused. Be a sponge for learning. Build your confidence. Find your passion. Improve your speed, and, one final thought...

Every day I count my blessings and am grateful for all of the good things in my life. Part of your blessings and gratitude should include your uniqueness and the gifts the good Lord has given you to use. Use them wisely in your life. Enjoy the ride, and as I say to all my friends: "Stay close."

My best,

Leo

P.S.: Oh, by the way, what is YOUR value?

mirror mirror on the wall
am **i** the most <u>valued</u>
of them all?

Appendix

APPENDIX

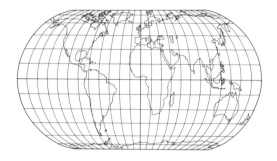

I've had the pleasure and privilege of coaching top FEs from around the world where many cultural differences exist. We share many similarities in our challenges to compete on our value and distinguish ourselves to our clients around the globe.

Clients around the world are changing in similar ways. They are more sophisticated and have more competitive options. In reaction, we must distinguish ourselves on our value, and have world-class answers to the seven questions on the Value Ladder. They are global, universally appropriate and applicable.

To assist our global readers with their challenges to distinguish themselves with their compelling story of value, we are pleased to share a sampling of our Value Ladder language translations.

The Value Ladder™ in English

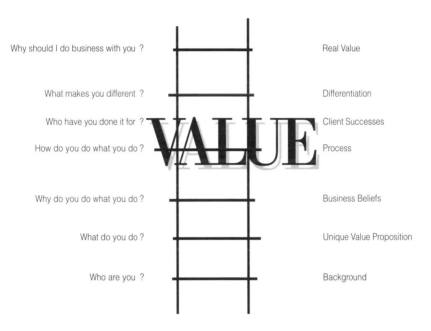

Why should I do business with you ?	Real Value
What makes you different ?	Differentiation
Who have you done it for ?	Client Successes
How do you do what you do ?	Process
Why do you do what you do ?	Business Beliefs
What do you do ?	Unique Value Proposition
Who are you ?	Background

The Valuc Ladder™ in Spanish

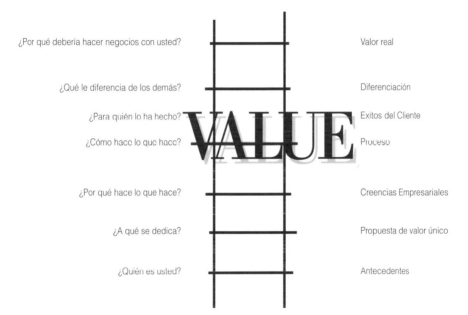

¿Por qué debería hacer negocios con usted?	Valor real
¿Qué le diferencia de los demás?	Diferenciación
¿Para quién lo ha hecho?	Exitos del Cliente
¿Cómo hace lo que hace?	Proceso
¿Por qué hace lo que hace?	Creencias Empresariales
¿A qué se dedica?	Propuesta de valor único
¿Quién es usted?	Antecedentes

The Value Ladder™ in French

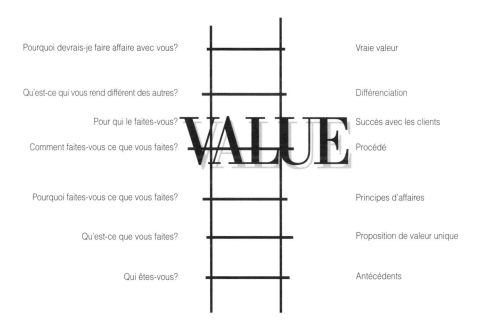

Pourquoi devrais-je faire affaire avec vous?   Vraie valeur

Qu'est-ce qui vous rend différent des autres?   Différenciation

Pour qui le faites-vous?   Succès avec les clients

Comment faites-vous ce que vous faites?   Procédé

Pourquoi faites-vous ce que vous faites?   Principes d'affaires

Qu'est-ce que vous faites?   Proposition de valeur unique

Qui êtes-vous?   Antécédents

The Value Ladder™ in German

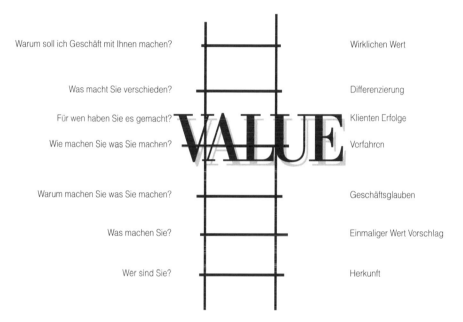

Warum soll ich Geschäft mit Ihnen machen?	Wirklichen Wert
Was macht Sie verschieden?	Differenzierung
Für wen haben Sie es gemacht?	Klienten Erfolge
Wie machen Sie was Sie machen?	Vorfahren
Warum machen Sie was Sie machen?	Geschäftsglauben
Was machen Sie?	Einmaliger Wert Vorschlag
Wer sind Sie?	Herkunft

The Value Ladder™ in Italian

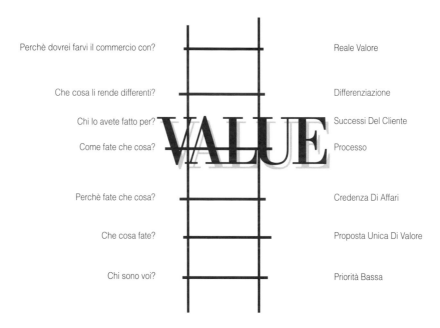

Perchè dovrei farvi il commercio con? Reale Valore

Che cosa li rende differenti? Differenziazione

Chi lo avete fatto per? Successi Del Cliente

Come fate che cosa? Processo

Perchè fate che cosa? Credenza Di Affari

Che cosa fate? Proposta Unica Di Valore

Chi sono voi? Priorità Bassa

The Value Ladder™ in Portuguese

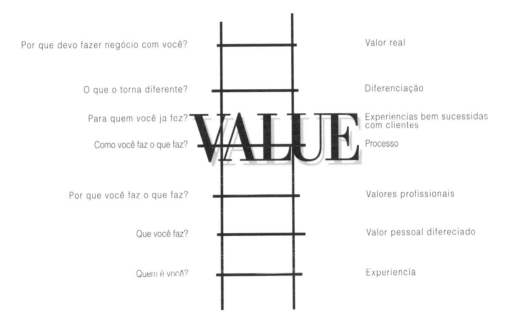

Por que devo fazer negócio com você? — Valor real

O que o torna diferente? — Diferenciação

Para quem você ja fez? — Experiencias bem sucessidas com clientes

Como você faz o que faz? — Processo

Por que você faz o que faz? — Valores profissionais

Que você faz? — Valor pessoal difereciado

Quem é você? — Experiencia

The Value Ladder™ in Hebrew

תמורה אמיתית

הבחנה

הצלחות אצל לקוחו

תהליך

השקפות עסקיות

הצעת תמורה ייחודי

רקע

מדוע כדאי לי לעשות אתך עסקים?

מה מבדיל אותך מאחרים?

עבור מי עסקת בכך?

כיצד את/ה עוסק/ת בכך?

מדוע את/ה עוסק/ת בכך?

במה את/ה עוסק/ת?

מי את/ה?

The Value Ladder™ in Arabic

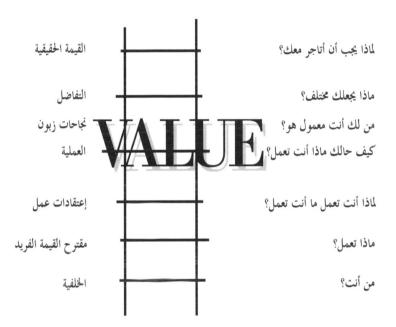

القيمة الحقيقية	لماذا يجب أن أتاجر معك؟
التفاضل	ماذا يجعلك مختلف؟
نجاحات زبون	من لك أنت معمول هو؟
العملية	كيف حالك ماذا أنت تعمل؟
إعتقادات عمل	لماذا أنت تعمل ما أنت تعمل؟
مقترح القيمة الفريد	ماذا تعمل؟
الخلفية	من أنت؟

The Value Ladder™ in Russian

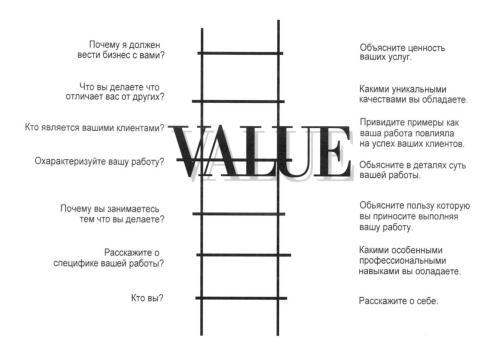

Почему я должен
вести бизнес с вами?

Объясните ценность
ваших услуг.

Что вы делаете что
отличает вас от других?

Какими уникальными
качествами вы обладаете.

Кто является вашими клиентами?

Привидите примеры как
ваша работа повлияла
на успех ваших клиентов.

Охарактеризуйте вашу работу?

Обьясните в деталях суть
вашей работы.

Почему вы занимаетесь
тем что вы делаете?

Обьясните пользу которую
вы приносите выполняя
вашу работу.

Расскажите о
специфике вашей работы?

Какими особенными
профессиональными
навыками вы ооладаете.

Кто вы?

Расскажите о себе.

Need More Help in Discovering and Articulating Your Value?

If you've enjoyed reading, *Mirror, Mirror on the Wall...Am I the Most Valued of Them All?* and are ready to go to the next step in becoming the best you can be, please contact us for more information.

Many of the quotes we've sourced can be found in some of our favorite books on the topic of value. A complimentary list of those books we believe can enhance your knowledge and understanding of the value revolution, and how to distinguish yourself in a crowded marketplace, is yours for the asking.

For additional information on our programs, services and customized solutions, contact:

Pusateri Consulting and Training, LLC
6255 Sheridan Drive
Suite 100
Williamsville, NY 14221
+1.716.631.9860 V
+1.716.631-9471 F
www.pusatericonsulting.com
leo@pusatericonsulting.com

Empowering Organizations And Individuals To Discover And Articulate Their Unique Value